THE LANGUAGE OF MEDITATION

Studies of four major nineteenth-century novelists —
Jane Austen, George Eliot, George Meredith, and
Henry James. Professor Halperin examines each
author's conception of the human mental processes
and demonstrates that each of the writers he examines
uses the secular meditation as a vehicle for the
self-revelation of his or her protagonist. Their
understanding of others and of external reality is
generally impaired, prior to the meditation, by the
short-sightedness of egoism. In each of the novels
examined in this work it is the act of meditation that
opens the way for the heroine to self-knowledge. The
argument provides analyses of the nature of these
meditations, the narrative language employed to
articulate them, and the moral importance of the
relationship between the heroine and the chief male
protagonist.

THE LANGUAGE

OF

MEDITATION

FOUR STUDIES IN NINETEENTH-CENTURY FICTION

JOHN HALPERIN
(University of Southern California)

ARTHUR H. STOCKWELL LTD.
Elms Court   Ilfracombe
Devon

SBN 7223 0378 - 5
PRINTED IN GREAT BRITAIN BY
ARTHUR H. STOCKWELL LTD.
Elms Court   -   Ilfracombe
Devon

75 - 150236

CONTENTS

To My Father

*who first inspired in me
desire for knowledge
and respect for truth*

FOREWORD

Jane Austen, George Eliot, George Meredith, and Henry James each had his or her own image of the human mental processes – of the way the human mind works – and the image of each is demonstrably different from that of the others. This is a major theme of my study, which attempts to provide a constant in the comparative examination of the four writers by focussing on a series of similar meditation scenes in seven of their novels. Examination of these scenes illuminates to some extent the ways in which the four authors conceive of the epistemological process requisite in the course of their protagonists' "education", an education in the art of moral vision. In each case, what is emphasized is that the writer's perspective, the way he or she imagines the human mind to be, is always reflected to some extent in the narrative structure peculiar to the particular novel.

It is a great pleasure to acknowledge thankfully the help and encouragement of a number of people. I am particularly grateful to Professor J. Hillis Miller of Yale University, who read this study in manuscript several times and made many invaluable suggestions. I am also indebted to Professors David V. Erdman and Richard A. Levine of the State University of New York at Stony Brook for their careful reading of the manuscript and their many helpful comments. I should like to thank Professor Earl R. Wasserman of The Johns Hopkins University for his very useful criticism of my discussion of Jane Austen. I am also grateful to Professor Charles R. Anderson of Johns Hopkins, whose comments on some of the similarities between

7

Elizabeth Bennet in *Pride and Prejudice* and Isabel Archer in *The Portrait of A Lady* provided the *donnée* for this study, and who also contributed some useful comments on my treatment of James. I am very much indebted to Professor Howard Schultz of Southern Illinois University for early help and advice, to Professor Irving Ribner, late of Stony Brook, for more recent encouragement, and to Professor Dale Underwood, late of the University of New Hampshire, for his inspiring qualities as a teacher. And I would like to express my gratitude to my parents for their unceasing confidence.

I should also like to thank the staffs of the Enoch Pratt Free Library of Baltimore and the Milton S. Eisenhower Library at The Johns Hopkins University for help in getting books needed for this project, and the Graduate School of the State University of New York at Stony Brook for a grant-in-aid for the preparation of this manuscript for the press.

And finally, I am indebted to Mr. James Stewart, Mr. Michael Safdi, and the undergraduate residents of Baker House, Johns Hopkins University, 1966-1969, for their moral and other support during the interesting period of my residence in Baltimore.

The writing of this book was facilitated in part by a National Defense Education Act Fellowship.

John Halperin

Manhattan Beach,
California

CHAPTER ONE

INTRODUCTION

This study will focus on similar scenes in seven novels by four writers. The writers are Jane Austen, George Eliot, George Meredith, and Henry James. The novels are *Pride and Prejudice, Emma, Middlemarch, Daniel Deronda, The Egoist, The Portrait of A Lady,* and *The Golden Bowl.* The scenes in question are what I have chosen to label "meditation" scenes, by which I do not mean scenes in which there occurs any formally structured religious meditation, but rather scenes in which the novel's heroine sees herself in relation to others clearly for the first time. Such new insight usually leads in turn to an increase in self-knowledge and thence to a more objective view of others. The meditations, in a word, are secular. In each instance the newfound intensity of self-awareness is reached through a dislocation of some relationship with another person, usually the man with whom the heroine has in some way been paired in the course of the novel's action.

All four writers deal consistently with the psychological processes, with the inner reality of their characters, which in these novels becomes embodied in the "education" that comes with increased self-knowledge. In attempting to find the similarities and differences in their perspectives upon and methods of revealing the mental processes of human beings, I have, in the following chapters, used the meditation scene as the *constant,* as mathematicians might say — that is, something which may always be identified in the works of the four writers and which may serve as a point of departure for comparison. Each elaborate retrospective meditation, for example, signals a climactic moment in the heroine's movement from self-absorption to self-discovery. In each scene the heroine, who is always the sentient center of the novel, meditates at some length about a man she is either about to marry, or has just escaped marrying, or will marry eventually, or is already married to. In each case the woman reflecting sees her relationship to this man altered in some basic way from what it had been before, sees herself with a new objectivity, and expresses her thoughts to herself at some length. In a scene devoid of dialogue or any physical action, she looks within herself, perceives or begins to perceive elements of her real nature to which she had previously been blind, and moves toward a more thorough understanding of those personal relationships the dislocation of which has caused such convulsive psychic reassessment in the first place. What is always dramatically represented is the climax of "education", of self-discovery. I intend to show, in dealing with each of these passages, what the analysis of such a passage may tell the reader about the novel in which it appears and about the author who wrote it, and what its relationship is to the other passages I have chosen to consider.

My method will be to work from the inside out, showing first how the passage's meaning may be extrapolated from its linguistic construction, and then how the passage in question is related to the overall meaning of the novel and to the imagination which created the novel. Before deciding what the role of the particular scene may be in the novel as a whole, I shall ask, in each case, this question: How, according to the author, does the human mind work? What sort of language does the narrator use to describe the thoughts of the character who is meditating, and what will the answer to this question tell the reader about the author's conception of the mental processes of human beings? I think that this question of narrative language is an important one and that it has all too often been ignored. If one accepts the statement, as I do, that every novel in fact *has* a narrative voice of some sort, then quite obviously a comparison of the similarities and differences among the narrative voices of several different novelists will seem interesting and valuable. How close is the narrator to the action he describes? How much does he know, and how much of what he knows does he tell? What kind of language does he use? These questions, while perhaps not always directly related to the meditation motif itself, nevertheless need sometimes to be taken into consideration; for the language in which a character's thoughts are related, the vantage-point from which they are related, the relative completeness of their presentation — these things are all inseparable from the central question of the significance and meaning of a particular character's thoughts. The content of thought and the way in which it is expressed to the reader are, after all, interdependent things — are, in fact, the same thing, just as form and meaning are always symbiotic in all literature.

The question of the ontological basis of voice in fiction is one that cannot be fully treated here, but some of the problems inherent in dealing with any narrative voice need, at the very least I should think, to be touched upon, however briefly. In any novel the voice one hears or encounters in it results from the conjunction of several entities. In any passage, for example, in which one encounters the thoughts of a fictional personage, the language used to give expression to those thoughts must necessarily be a mixture of several different things. At the lowest level, one must take into account the character himself, whose mind, at least as the narrator and the author perceive it, is inevitably one of the shaping forces of the language. The language, in other words, results partly from those thoughts themselves and is thus never wholly separable from the imaginary mind thinking. At the next level there is the mind of the narrator, a mind which, at least in the usually omnisciently narrated nineteenth-century novel, completely surrounds the minds of the characters in the novel. The language of indirect discourse or interior monologue, then, is always contingent to varying degrees not only upon the mind of the fictional personage, but also upon the mind which perceives that mind and relates those thoughts to the reader through the refracting medium of its own mind. The mind of the narrator in such novels, then, may be described as a sort of ubiquitous consciousness, an all-surrounding mind through which the reader is allowed to perceive, more or less clearly, the mind of the protagonist. For the mind of the narrator may be close to or far away from the mind of the character, and it may vary in its degree of opacity. At some times it — and thus the reader — perceives and understands more than at other times. And yet, despite these questions of distance and clarity, the mind of the narrator is never wholly absent or detached, for the reader is always aware, to varying extents, that the minds of the characters come through to him only through the ubiquitous filtering presence of the narrator's mind.

Beyond these two levels of consciousness, it seems, there are two higher minds to consider if one is concerned with the ontology of voice in fiction: these are the minds of the author and the reader. However many levels of consciousness one may wish to identify in any novel, the indisputable fact is always, of course, that the novel itself is only the product of the mind of the author, and that the narrator and the character exist only in the language of the novel as it was written by that author. The author, it must be assumed, has some sort of distanced perspective both on his narrator and his character — assuming, as I have said, that one is willing to accept the existence of a narrator who is an entity separate from the author. And finally, beyond all of these other levels of consciousness, there is the consciousness of the reader, a consciousness which is of course necessary to the reading of the novel itself. The consciousness of the reader is always important, for in the very act of reading the reader himself, because of whatever prejudices or concerns he may have, helps give shape to those other consciousnesses he encounters. He reads things in a particular way peculiar to himself and to his own mind, and in doing so is partly responsible for their existence in the first place. The consciousnesses of the author, narrator, and protagonist, in other words, are always dependent to some extent upon the way in which they are perceived by the reader.

The ontological basis of voice and the language which gives it existence, then, is the result of the coalescence of four consciousnesses — those of the reader, the author, the narrator, and the fictional personage whose thoughts are under scrutiny. Thus if one asks, as he is likely to do in the following pages of this study and perhaps others like it, whose language he encounters in passages of indirect discourse or interior monologue, the answer would seem to be that the language is a result of these four simultaneous levels of consciousness, and that it can be attributed wholly to none of them separately. The voice which is the source of that language, then, results from the simultaneous copresence of several minds, and thus the voice itself belongs wholly to no one alone but rather to several different entities, all of which together, in varying degrees, provide the language which that voice speaks. It seems to me that these considerations are important ones in the context of what follows in succeeding chapters, much of which is an attempt to analyze the meanings of various passages which deal in depth with the consciousnesses of the protagonists and the narrative structure within which these consciousnesses are examined.

The meditation in fiction is of course not a phenomenon unique to nineteenth-century novelists, nor is the analysis of mental states of fictional characters unique in the fiction of any period. Richardson, Smollett, Sterne, and Scott, among others, were also preoccupied with the phenomena of consciousness and self-consciousness. In addition to the four writers I have chosen to consider, other nineteenth-century writers such as the Brontë sisters, Thackeray, Trollope, and Hardy were also quite obviously interested in the psychology of their characters, and the subject has of course been taken over by many twentieth-century writers as their own. But there seems to me to be a particular continuity among Jane Austen, George Eliot, Meredith, and James, a continuity not just among their themes but among their methods of rendering them. There are important differences too, of course, but the similarity in situation and general construction of the meditations I propose to consider especially invites this comparative approach.

The meditation as a vehicle of self-discovery, as a measurement of the different ways the four writers in question view the human mental processes, as an index to at least a partial understanding of the narrative structure of their novels — these are the themes of this study.

II

In his brilliant study, *Mimesis: The Representation of Reality in Western Literature* (1946), Erich Auerbach argues that the source of a writer's style may often be found in his historical and social milieu. His thesis is that a man's style and his cultural environment inevitably interact. Auerbach's book, which is in effect a history of narrative fiction, is constructed upon the following methodological premise: analyze a random passage in a novel and it will tell you something about the novel's totality and also about the immediate milieu in which it was written. Auerbach demonstrates that various strategies of language and rhetoric are the means by which different ages can be distinguished from one another in their grasp and presentation of daily, external reality.

My approach to the novels under consideration here is somewhat similar to Auerbach's, with two important exceptions. First, I make no pretense of randomness. The passages I have chosen to analyze have been carefully selected, for reasons already enumerated. Second, my focus will not be on the novel's or the novelist's grasp and presentation of daily, external reality, but rather on his grasp and presentation of psychological, inner reality. Critics have often commented, for example, on George Eliot's firsthand acquaintance with the quotidian reality of English provincial life, or on her own comparison of her craft with Dutch *genre*-painting.[1] What has sometimes been neglected, however, is her familiarity with and conception of the *inner* states of human beings.

I am not so much concerned here with mimesis in the manner of Auerbach and W.J. Harvey as I am with *autonomy* in the manner of Ortega y Gasset.[2] The former deal with fiction as the representation of external reality, the latter with fiction as the representation of an autonomous, inner reality. In the second case the material of the novel is imaginary psychology, and the novelist's sphere of observation is that of the psychological processes of real people. It is this second perspective from which, for the most part, I shall be viewing these novels.

And yet I do not mean to imply that mimesis and autonomy are terms mutually exclusive, or that they refer to ineluctably separate categories of literary procedure. Although I have characterized the methodology of this study as that more nearly approaching the assumption of autonomy, it is clear that neither concept makes sense without the other — means, in fact, nothing unless the other is taken into consideration. For autonomy is itself a form of mimesis. If the autonomous novel does not imitate an existing reality, it imitates an inner one, one necessarily divorced from ordinary life. In a purely autonomous novel the author interests and entraps his reader in the smaller world of his imagination, constricting his horizon rather than widening it. Such a novel frees the reader from his world and allows him to transmigrate to the world of the novel itself — and then keeps him there, prohibiting him from returning to his own world. The novel's illusion of reality must never be interrupted. Thus "thesis" novels and historical novels, for example — those dealing with politics, economics, or social theory — can never be purely autonomous, as Ortega points out. The novel must provide a world of its own if it is to be purely autonomous, and thus it cannot also propagate moral and philosophical systems. The autonomous novel makes the reader care more for the imagined world than the real one, and he must perceive that imagined world from within and feel surrounded by it. Where specifically, then, is the connecting link between mimesis and autonomy? It is in the paradox that the autonomous novel is incompatible with outer reality principally because it is itself a realistic *genre,* a *genre* of inner reality. In establishing that inner reality it must abolish the outer one.[3]

III

The interest of all four of these writers in the psychology of their characters is only one way in which they are similar. Of course they are different in many ways too, and in following chapters I shall be pointing out how they are both similar to and different from one another. But one could make several generalizations about the novels of all four writers, generalizations which, since they would interrupt the progress of discussions in succeeding chapters, I shall mention briefly here. The four writers, in addition to their interest in the psychological processes of their characters, share, for example, intense moral preoccupations — often with money; *Persuasion, Silas Marner, The Egoist,* and *The Portrait of A Lady* are all novels about money, for instance. All four novelists might be identified by Lionel Trilling as novelists of manners; that is, they are concerned with manners as a reflection of morals, and thus their novels, with very few exceptions indeed, are set preponderantly in drawing-rooms and studies — inside houses rather than outside of them. All four writers are fond of using the Cinderella motif, as one can see from *Mansfield Park, The Mill on the Floss, The Ordeal of Richard Feverel,* and, to take just one example from James, *The Wings of the Dove.* In terms of technique, there are other similarities. All four writers prefer the indirection of dramatization in order to preserve the "illusion of reality" in their novels — George Eliot and Meredith less so, it may be, than Jane Austen and James. All sought for economy of composition and attempted to root out of their novels whatever failed to contribute to the dominant thematic concerns — though Meredith was perhaps less successful in this regard than the others. James's dictum in his preface to *The Ambassadors* that fiction is comprised of scenes and preparations for scenes — and that whatever is not scene is picture — is a critical principle applied as easily to *Emma, Daniel Deronda,* and *The Egoist* as to *The Golden Bowl* or *The Ambassadors* itself. All four writers view language as an index to behavior — how people express themselves helps determine what kind of people they are (Mr Collins in *Pride and Prejudice,* Mrs. Poyser in *Adam Bede,* Dr. Middleton in *The Egoist,* Mrs. Lowder in *The Wings of the Dove).* In many of the novels of all four writers the point of view is limited for the most part to that of a "central consciousness", and thus the theme of the education of the protagonist becomes fundamental *(Emma, The Mill on the Floss, The Ordeal of Richard Feverel, The Ambassadors,* just to mention a few examples).

Jane Austen's Willoughbys and Middletons reappear, perhaps more than in name only, in *The Egoist,* and the subjects

of her novels are not wholly different from those treated by
Thackeray, Trollope, George Eliot, Meredith, and James,
among others. In method and range of interests she is more
like James, it may be, than she is like any of the others,[4] and
this fact may well be what prompted Virginia Woolf to write
that, had Jane Austen lived longer, she would have been a
forerunner not only of James himself but of Proust as well.[5]
And yet James's greatest literary debt, at least among the
English novelists, seems to have been not to Jane Austen but
to George Eliot. He wrote during his lifetime nine different
essays on or reviews of George Eliot's novels, stories, and
poems — more than he wrote about any other novelist except
Hawthorne, whom James made the subject of a full-length
study in 1879.[6] George Eliot in her turn was profoundly
influenced by Thackeray and attempted to emulate his
combination of realism and philosophical commentary. The
multitude of connections and cross-influences among the
nineteenth-century novelists helps explain the many
similarities in theme and construction one is so likely to find
in their novels, and I shall not attempt in this study to define
and assess all the difficult problems of "influence", as if
literary history were linear or deterministic, a process toward
increasing complexity and sophistication. It would be more
profitable, I think, simply to view these nineteenth-century
authors as a constellation of novelists writing more or less at
the same time, within the same general tradition, each doing
something unique with the conventions, themes, and
techniques of that tradition. The mere fact that these authors
are writing more or less within the same literary tradition
should, I would hope, make their essentially different
conceptions of the human mind and its modes of operation
that much more striking and interesting.

[1] See *Adam Bede*, Chapter XVII.

[2] See Harvey's *Character and the Novel* (1965), and Ortega's "Notes on the
Novel" in *The Dehumanization of Art* (1925).

[3] For further discussion of this theoretical paradox, originally proposed, I believe,
by Ortega, see his essay, cited above.

[4] These affinities have only occasionally been pointed out. See, for example. F.R.
Leavis, *The Great Tradition* (1948); A. Walton Litz, *Jane Austen: A Study of Her
Artistic Development* (1965), probably the most intelligent treatment to date of
Jane Austen's novels; Irène Simon, "Jane Austen and *The Art of the Novel,*" *ES*

(1962); and Virginia Woolf, "Jane Austen at Sixty", a review of Chapman's edition of the novels (see Chapter 2, n.2) in the *Nation*, December 15, 1923.

[5] See "Jane Austen at Sixty".

[6] See Chapter 5 for a fuller discussion of this topic.

CHAPTER TWO

JANE AUSTEN (1775 - 1817)

The brilliance of *Pride and Prejudice* (1813) results in part
from its narrative technique. The reader, in his judgments of
the novel's characters and their actions, is often limited by
the author to the point of view of Elizabeth Bennet. She is
the novel's "center of consciousness", and the reader is
invited, at least during the first half of the story, to share her
vision. Since *Pride and Prejudice* provides no other sustained
perspective on the action, the reader must supply his own if
he is to avoid Elizabeth's prejudices. Jane Austen's irony here
is neither detached nor self-defensive, as Marvin Mudrick
would have us believe, but is rather directed at the reader as
well as at the characters themselves.[1] When Elizabeth finally
discovers how proud, prejudiced, and therefore mistaken her
judgment has been,[2] many readers of *Pride and Prejudice* find
that they must acknowledge the same things about themselves, for Jane Austen has invited us throughout the first
half of the novel to identify ourselves with the heroine and to
share at least some of her illusions. Elizabeth, of course, is
not the narrator of the novel, but in its early sections and in
many of its later ones she is undeniably its sentient center,
and as such she is patently "unreliable", to use Wayne Booth's
word.[3] The heroine's position is always established as the
point of view in Jane Austen's novels, a point of view,
however, usually within the surrounding, though sometimes
effaced, perspective of the ubiquitous narrator. But the
narrator, despite his omniscience, is not blatantly intrusive,
and this is why the point of view in *Pride and Prejudice*, for
perhaps the first time in Jane Austen's work, is "unreliable".
The reader, because of his partial identification with the
heroine, is likely to find himself sharing some of Elizabeth's
prejudices, and thus her ultimate self-discovery may also be

partially his own.

Several other radical elements of Jane Austen's art need to be identified before we examine the crucial meditation scene in *Pride and Prejudice*. The language used by the characters in her novels is often an index to behavior.[4] A character's syntax, his use or overuse of tropes, his diction in general — all these help tell what he is. Style is the man, and obscure or inappropriate diction will often signal some dangerous moral aberration. Jane Austen's writing, for example, is consistently unmetaphorical. The unmetaphorical nature of her prose is one of several affinities her writing has with the eighteenth century; there is also the use of conceptual or abstract nouns, the many generalizations and elegant epigrams, the balanced antitheses and oppositions, and the reserve and decorum of tone.[5] And yet, Jane Austen has not just one but rather several styles.[6] There is the Johnsonian style I have been talking about; there is the pre-Romantic style of sensibility; and there is the ordinary, idiomatic language of the Regency period. There is also something else of vital importance in Jane Austen's prose, a phenomenon which is not so much a style of writing as it is a method of rendering the mental states of protagonists. This is the language of indirect interior monologue, in which the authorial or narrative voice continuously present guides the reader through the character's consciousness.[7] A good deal of Jane Austen's prose is omniscient description, wherein the narrator's focus is the mind of the protagonist, and the prose itself, usually Johnsonian, is a narrative description of what is going on within that mind. Jane Austen was interested in the effects of events on the mind, and thus her novels, with their "centers of consciousness", are in large measure histories of an education in values. It is the educational process, the inquiry into the nature of true and false values, that stimulates meditation in Jane Austen's characters. The education of the protagonist usually results in a final realization of the evils of excessive subjectivity. The character moves in these climactic scenes from blind self-interest to self-knowledge, and from self-knowledge to a more objective view both of himself and of the society in which he lives.

For Jane Austen, as subsequent passages from both *Pride*

and Prejudice and *Emma* should demonstrate, this movement toward a more complete moral vision may be convulsive, nervous, and even abrupt, but the protagonist usually remains articulate and logical in her crisis. Despite a bombardment of new ideas— even of revelations — the language used to describe these experiences is usually abstract and literal, elegantly balanced and cool. Regardless of the intelligence and rationality of Jane Austen's heroines, however, they remain self-deceived a good deal of the time because of their egoism, a phenomenon which helps create the sustained irony of presentation in the novels. These facts will be more fully evident shortly.

I

Pride and Prejudice represents a substantial artistic advance over *Sense and Sensibility* (1811). In the latter, Jane Austen constructs an instructive dichotomy by making Elinor, her heroine, an exemplum and apostle of sense, and Marianne, Elinor's sister, an illustration of the pitfalls and unhappiness attendant upon excessive sensibility. The author uses two characters to represent the two states she is interested in defining, and this is where the major artistic weakness lies. In her later and better novels, most of the contradictions and conflicts are combined in *one* character, and that character is thus rendered more interesting and believable. Emma, it will be seen, is snobbish, conceited, egotistical, and occasionally stupid, yet she is also gracious, loving, loyal, and generally intelligent, and this is what makes her fascinating. Edmund Wilson's famous complaint about Dickens — that he could not get the good and the bad together in one character and that his characters were thus almost all one-dimensional and unbelievable — is a complaint that might also be made about some of the characters in *Sense and Sensibility*, but not those of *Emma*, written five years later.[8]

In *Pride and Prejudice* the reader can see this process — that is, the process of investing characters with several contradictory traits, thus making them more credible — beginning to emerge.[9] After reading *Sense and Sensibility* one might expect that the two major characters in *Pride and Prejudice*, Elizabeth and Darcy, would also represent specific concepts or values. And such, in the novel's early chapters, appears to be the case. Darcy seems exceedingly proud, while Elizabeth is immediately prejudiced against him because of his initial indifference to her. She turns her attention instead to his enemy Wickham, who continually gratifies her ego with elaborate homage. The reader may perhaps sense more clearly than Elizabeth does that Wickham is a gilded coin and not pure gold, but he is undeniably prejudiced along with Elizabeth against Darcy and what seems to be that gentleman's debilitating pride. Yet Elizabeth's prejudice is itself a result of a different kind of pride — pride in her own supposedly unassailable judgment. She also takes pride in what she feels is the superiority of her social sense over that of her sister Jane, whose naïve social judgment is nevertheless more accurate, on occasion, than Elizabeth's own; and in what she feels is her precedence over her friend Charlotte Lucas, who makes a *mariage de convenance* which appalls Elizabeth, but who nevertheless has the audacity later on to be happy or at least satisfied in it. Elizabeth's self-assurance, her confidence in her own intellect, her anger at Darcy's apparent indifference to her — in short her *pride* — are the roots of her prejudice. And Darcy's pride is also part and parcel of prejudice: he is prejudiced against the Bennets, and specifically against Jane as a suitable match for his friend Bingley; his tastes in music and literature seem somewhat prejudiced — so does his taste in women, at least for a while; he is prejudiced against families engaged in trade and in favor of those who own large property; and he seems satisfied only by the most restrained, decorous sort of behavior. What is this after all but pride — pride in himself, in his family, and in his property? Class prejudice, which is the source of much of Darcy's pride, is justifiable to some extent for Jane Austen, but extreme pride — so extreme that it seems at times to deny the possibility of any kind of humane behavior — she inevitably condemns.

Both Elizabeth and Darcy thus have both pride and prejudice, yet by the end of the novel Elizabeth's prejudice against Darcy is put in the wrong by his generous behavior, while his excessive pride and restraint tend to recede under the influence of his love for her; and of course the novel ends in the synthesis of a perfect marriage. Darcy has been wrong, but not as wrong as Elizabeth has believed; Elizabeth has been blind — and so has the reader to some extent — until she is undeceived by Darcy's letter. It is the chapter following the one in which she receives and reads the letter which will be my focus.

The scene occurs during Elizabeth's visit to Charlotte Lucas Collins in Kent. Elizabeth and Darcy have been thrown together several times at the nearby residence of his aunt, Lady Catherine de Bourgh, and Elizabeth has, as she thinks, no reason to alter her original prejudice against Darcy: he is still proud, and furthermore he has treated shamefully, she still believes, her friend Wickham. Thus she is quite naturally surprised when he proposes to her, patronizingly, and rudely rejects him with charges of insufferable and obnoxious pride, prejudice against her family and specifically against her sister Jane, and dishonorable treatment of his former dependent Wickham. Darcy, on his part, has been captivated by Elizabeth's beauty, her wit, and her emancipated intellect, but retreats in the face of her scornful refusal behind his habitual pride and reserve, and the two take an unpromising leave. The next day Elizabeth receives the letter from Darcy, and her reaction to it constitutes what I believe to be one of the central passages of the novel. He explains his past behavior logically; Elizabeth reads the letter carefully. Her first reaction is that it is all humbug; her second reaction is that parts of it must undeniably be true; if parts, then all, and she is finally convinced that she has misjudged Darcy. Elizabeth puts the letter down, and there follows a passage, or rather a series of related passages, which together form an elaborate retrospective meditation; the entire chapter deals with the processes of her mind.

In this perturbed state of mind, with thoughts that could rest on nothing, she walked on; but it would not do; in half a minute the letter was unfolded again, and collecting herself as well as she could, she again began the mortifying perusal of all that related to Wickham, and commanded herself so far as to examine the meaning of every sentence. (1) The account of his connection with the Pemberley family was exactly what he had related himself; and the kindness of the late Mr. Darcy, though she had not before known its extent, agreed equally well with his own words. (2) So far each recital confirmed the other; but when she came to the will, the difference was great. (3) What Wickham

had said of the living was fresh in her memory, and as she recalled his
very words, it was impossible not to feel that there was gross duplicity
on one side or the other; and for a few moments, she flattered herself
that her wishes did not err.(4) But when she read and re-read with the
closest attention, the particulars immediately following of Wickham's
resigning all pretensions to the living, of his receiving in lieu so consider-
able a sum as three thousand pounds, again she was forced to hesitate.
(5) She put down the letter, weighed every circumstance with what she
meant to be impartiality — deliberated on the probability of each
statement — but with little success.(6) On both sides it was only
assertion.(7) Again she read on; but every line proved more clearly that
the affair, which she had believed it impossible that any contrivance
could so represent as to render Mr. Darcy's conduct in it less than
infamous, was capable of a turn which must make him entirely
blameless throughout the world.(8)

*   *   *   *   *   *   *

She perfectly remembered everything that had passed in conversation
between Wickham and herself, in their first evening at Mr. Philips's.
Many of his expressions were still fresh in her memory. She was *now*
struck with the impropriety of such communications to a stranger, and
wondered it had escaped her before. She saw the indelicacy of putting
himself forward as he had done, and the inconsistency of his professions
with his conduct. She remembered that he had boasted of having no
fear of seeing Mr. Darcy, that Mr. Darcy might leave the country, but
that he should stand his ground: yet he had avoided the Netherfield ball
the very next week. She remembered also that, till the Netherfield
family had quitted the country, he had told his story to no one but
herself; but that after their removal it had been everywhere discussed;
that he had then no reserves, no scruples in sinking Mr. Darcy's
character, though he had assured her that respect for the father would
always prevent his exposing the son.

*   *   *   *   *   *   *

Every lingering struggle in Wickham's favour grew fainter and fainter;
and in further justification of Mr. Darcy, she could not but allow that
Mr. Bingley, when questioned by Jane, had long ago asserted his
blamelessness in the affair; that proud and repulsive as were his manners,
she had never, in the whole course of their acquaintance — an
acquaintance which had latterly brought them much together, and
given her a sort of intimacy with his ways — seen anything that
betrayed him to be unprincipled or unjust — anything that spoke him of
irreligious or immoral habits; that among his own connections he was
esteemed and valued — that even Wickham had allowed him merit as a
brother, and that she had often heard him speak so affectionately of
his sister as to prove him capable of some amiable feeling; that had his
actions been what Wickham represented them, so gross a violation of
everything right could hardly have been concealed from the world; and
that friendship between a person capable of it, and such an amiable
man as Mr. Bingley, was incomprehensible.

*   *   *   *   *   *   *

She grew absolutely ashamed of herself. Of neither Darcy nor Wickham could she think without feeling that she had been blind, partial, prejudiced, absurd.

'How despicably have I acted!' she cried; 'I, who have prided myself on my discernment! I, who have valued myself on my abilities! who have often disdained the generous candour of my sister, and gratified my vanity in useless or blameable distrust. How humiliating is this discovery! yet, how just a humiliation! Had I been in love, I could not have been more wretchedly blind. But vanity, not love, has been my folly. Pleased with the preference of one, and offended by the neglect of the other, on the very beginning of our acquaintance, I have courted prepossession and ignorance, and driven reason away, where either were concerned. Till this moment I never knew myself.'10

These are selections — Elizabeth's meditation is actually much longer. In this chapter Elizabeth disbelieves everything in Darcy's letter at the beginning and accepts it as gospel at the end. And what happens to make her change her mind? Nothing. Nothing actually *happens* here — there are no new revelations of plot, there are no conversations, there are no external events of any kind. All that occurs in this chapter is that Elizabeth *thinks,* and in thinking changes her mind. The action is all mental action.

In the first three sections of the meditation quoted above, the narrator for the most part merely *tells* the reader what Elizabeth is doing and thinking; in the fourth part the narrative voice effaces itself to a greater extent, and the reader has more direct access to Elizabeth's thoughts, which are spoken out loud.

Elizabeth is in a "perturbed state of mind". She is unable to decide whether or not Darcy's letter is truthful; this is a serious matter, for if Darcy is telling the truth then Wickham is not, and all of her previous thoughts about the two of them are automatically invalidated and her judgment is proved faulty at every turn. Her perplexity is related by the omniscient narrator in concrete descriptive language; there is in these early sentences little alteration in the narrator's distance from the character he is describing. Elizabeth, says the narrator, is in the process of "collecting" and "commanding" herself so as to attempt to understand the letter objectively. The emphasis in this first section of the meditation is on Elizabeth's wavering judgment, her feeling that perhaps she is going to be proven wrong, her

"mortification" at the possibility, and her last struggle to
avoid the necessity of admitting error. This is the last time in
the novel that Elizabeth comes close to obfuscating the truth
(although, later on, she fails to see how completely Darcy has
remained in love with her). Thus, in sentence four, she flatters
herself "that her wishes did not err" and that perhaps she has
been right after all. And she attempts, as the sixth sentence
tells us, to weigh "every circumstance with what she means
to be impartiality" — a rather backward way of saying that
she has become aware of her prejudices and is now beginning
to lean the other way to balance them with some objectivity.

In the second section of the meditation Elizabeth is
"motionlessly seeing", to use a phrase of James's in his
preface to *The Portrait of A Lady* which also describes this
scene in *Pride and Prejudice*. The five sentences of the
paragraph begin similarly: "She perfectly remembered"; "She
was *now* struck"; "She saw"; "She remembered"; "She
remembered". There is no action here — not even any pacing
up and down or folding and unfolding of a letter; instead,
Elizabeth is reflecting, seeing her past actions in a new light,
that is, in the light of a present truth of which she is just now
in possession. Nothing physical *happens;* the movement here,
such as it is, is entirely mental. Yet in this section the narrator
is an obviously continuous presence. The past-tense narration
remains omniscient description. The "She saw", "She remembered" construction constantly reminds the reader that
everything he knows about Elizabeth's mind during these
moments is conveyed to him through the surrounding presence
of the narrative voice.

The third section of the meditation is all one sentence.
Jane Austen's narrator is using elaborate and complicated
sentence structure to express elaborate and complicated
thoughts. Assuming that language can be to some extent a
mirror-world of consciousness, that consciousness is more
often associative than logical, that thoughts and words are as
closely and inevitably connected as consciousness and
experience, then quite obviously language may reflect and
even help shape the content of experience. Kingsley, or Wilkie
Collins, or the early George Moore might have written the
passage this way: "Though Mr. Darcy had been indifferent, he

had never been rude. He was esteemed by his connections,
and his connections were too trustworthy to be doubted."
This is what this long passage tells the reader, but he would
not, of course, find in my simplified version any evidence of
Elizabeth's mental agony, which is what makes Jane Austen's
passage so striking and so forceful. She makes one see, or feel,
Elizabeth's lingering struggle, and she does this through the
language she provides her narrator.

In the fourth and last section of the meditation the
authorial voice is almost completely effaced (except for the
phrase "she cried") and the phenomenon of inner speech is
rendered dramatically through a soliloquy. This section
represents the climax not only of Elizabeth's meditation but
also of her education; here is her self-discovery, her recognition
of her own pride and prejudice: " 'Till this moment I never
knew myself' ".The passage emphasizes Elizabeth's pride in
her own "discernment", the inordinately high value she has
been putting on her "abilities", her "vanity", which she has
been at such pains to gratify, her "prepossession" and her
"ignorance", and the fact that she has been consistently at
work, thus far in the novel, at driving "reason away". It is
precisely these things that Elizabeth must realize if she is to
exorcise her egoism and see things as they really are. Thus one
might say that this scene is really the climax of the novel
itself; it occurs roughly in the middle, and everything that
follows is more or less a result of it, an unwinding of the knot,
a dénouement. In seeing clearly for the first time the nature
of Darcy, Elizabeth understands her own blindness and
irrationality for the first time also, and this discovery will in
turn enable her to relate to her family and friends with more
sympathy and understanding in subsequent sections of the
novel. It will also enable her and Darcy to come together at
last.

Elizabeth's meditation gives us Jane Austen's lessons:
appearances are deceiving, thus first impressions are not
always accurate;[11] pride and prejudice in human evaluation
are misleading; the egoism of subjectivity must therefore be
eradicated through the objectivity of rational judgment and
self-knowledge. The novel's central subject, after all, is the
education of its heroine, and it is in this that Elizabeth's

education begins to produce tangible results — she finally begins to see the errors she has made, errors due in large measure to blind self-interest, and thus she sees how mistaken her judgment has been all along.

In these passages Jane Austen's narrator remains for the most part a continuously surrounding presence. Elizabeth is rarely allowed to speak to the reader solely in her own voice; her thoughts are conveyed to us by the narrator most of the time. Her inner speech is reflected and perhaps refracted through the narrator's mind, which, while continuously present, is sometimes transparent enough to relate directly to the reader the content and mental rhythm of Elizabeth's mind as the narrator himself perceives them. What the content of Elizabeth's mind, as reflected through the narrator's, seems to tell us, is that while her thoughts may be the result of erroneous perception, due to egoism, her capacity for exercising rational and considered judgment is never seriously in doubt. While she may be irrational and easily prejudiced, she is at all times intelligent and articulate, even during the mental convulsion which she undergoes.

Even that convulsiveness is not enough, however, to dilute or enrich the literal, general, and abstract language used here with figurative language. On the contrary, the language here, as elsewhere in Jane Austen's fiction, remains singularly unfigurative. One might expect that when a character is bombarded suddenly by new ideas and personal revelations, he or she might see them, or some of them, in terms of visual images of some kind, for the human mind often does tend to incarnate experiential data into mental pictures. But this does not happen here; and perhaps we should not be surprised that this is so in a novel whose first sentence is as follows: "It is a truth universally acknowledged, that a single man in possession of a good fortune must be in want of a wife." The abstract and general qualities of Jane Austen's language remain with us throughout the novel, even in such a scene as the one just examined.

II

Emma (1816) is Jane Austen's best novel and one of the greatest in the language. Its greatness lies at its center — in

Emma herself. In *Sense and Sensibility* contradictory tendencies were embodied in contradictory persons. In *Pride and Prejudice* both titular transgressions were personified in the two major characters. In *Emma* it is Emma herself who embodies most of the contradictions and inconsistencies. Human beings are complex and unpredictable, capable of delighting one by surprising him; to compartmentalize people according to various arbitrary categories of personality (sense, sensibility, pride, prejudice) is to obfuscate their real natures. In Emma one may see clearly the human mental condition: the uncertainty, the egoism, the generosity, the self-delusion, the self-knowledge; all these, and a number of other warring tendencies as well, are radically present in this protagonist.

Emma, like Elizabeth Bennet, is another fictional "center of consciousness", and her education is once again the story of the novel. Emma's progress from the egoism of self-delusion and illusion to the objective "sympathy" of self-recognition and realistic perception is reflected in the novel's three movements — her collisions with Messrs. Elton, Churchill, and Knightley. Self-recognition is thus a theme here, as it is in *Pride and Prejudice*. Emma's mind is at the center of the novel, and in moving back and forth between it and its effects on others Jane Austen's story inevitably alternates between picture and scene, between exposition and drama.[12]

Emma's most serious mistake is her attempt to play God the Matchmaker. She is consistently wrong in her evaluations of the three male protagonists (just as Elizabeth misjudges both Darcy and Wickham), and the novel's ubiquitous irony thus comes in part, as Marvin Mudrick has said, from the "deceptiveness of surfaces".[13] The paramount theme of this novel, as of *Pride and Prejudice,* is self-deception in relation to judgments of others. Emma, like Elizabeth, trusts only her own judgment, and though much of it is sheer fancy she constantly feels the need to impose its conclusions on others. By the end of the novel she has discovered most of the blind spots in her own nature and thus, again like Elizabeth, is able to view others with more accuracy.

E.M. Forster has remarked that *all* of Jane Austen's characters are "round" or "capable of rotundity", meaning that all are unpredictable, three-dimensional, and capable of surprising the reader at any time.[14] Emma, obviously, is not all bad. She is certainly an egoist and a snob, but she also has the capacities to love and to be loyal.[15] She is intelligent and gregarious, and the reader is told that she is beautiful. She is not, despite her snobbishness, basically materialistic — she is more interested in people than in things. And she finally achieves a new toughness, a new honesty of mind, confronting as she does the ludicrousness of her earlier, more untutored conduct. She is often contrasted with Mr. Knightley, a man of both sense and feeling, logical and sympathetic; Emma is selfish and illogical until the end of the novel. *Emma* portrays Emma's progress from self-absorption to self-knowledge, as A.W. Litz rightly says; its story is its heroine's movement from selfishness to self-evaluation, a movement typical of Jane Austen's characters in general, including those in *Pride and Prejudice*. Emma, then, is to be both loved and judged.

Like Elizabeth Bennet, Emma is another "unreliable" sentient center of the novel. The major difference between them, however, is that in *Pride and Prejudice* we are sometimes taken in by Elizabeth's judgments of people and things. But in *Emma* we have, more consistently, two perspectives — that of Emma herself, whom we *know* to be in error (that is, unreliable) most of the time, and that of Jane Austen the "reliable" author, who has a constantly ironic perspective on her protagonist reminiscent, perhaps, of Swift's on Gulliver, though of course less acrimonious.[16] The author's ironic perspective on her protagonist is present in *Pride and Prejudice* too, but in that novel it is less ironic for reasons I shall explain shortly. The difference is one of degree and not of kind. Thus the reader of *Emma* is usually able to assess the protagonist with more success than he had in dealing with Elizabeth Bennet.

There are two very striking meditation scenes in *Emma*, similar in some ways to the one already examined in *Pride and Prejudice*. In *Pride and Prejudice* the construction of the meditation often took the "She saw", "She remembered" form; in *Emma* the third-person pronoun disappears a bit more often, and thus the narrative voice during the meditation

scenes becomes more frequently indistinguishable from that
of the character meditating. The reader has a harder time
discriminating between Emma's language and the narrator's.
And yet, as in *Pride and Prejudice,* the narrator's surrounding
presence is more or less continous; it is simply more
consistently transparent in *Emma.* This situation suggests an
interesting paradox. I have said that in *Emma* the narrative
perspective on the protagonist is more consistently ironic
than it is in *Pride and Prejudice,* and yet I have also said that
in *Emma* it becomes more often difficult to distinguish
between the narrator's voice and the character's. How can
this be? I think the explanation is that there are two modes
of irony simultaneously present in some sections of *Emma.*
The reader *knows* Emma to be in error throughout most of
the novel; there can be no question of her folly. In *Pride and
Prejudice* we are not aware of the full extent of Elizabeth's
mistakes until we know Darcy and Wickham better, and we
do not know them completely until Elizabeth does. But in
Emma there are few questions of this sort. Emma is wrong in
the Robert Martin affair; she is at fault in her dealings with
Mr. Elton; she is obtuse in her relationships with Jane
Fairfax and Frank Churchill; she is rude to Miss Bates; she
consistently fails to follow the excellent advice tendered her
by Mr. Knightley. She is snobbish, nosy, and pig-headed. We
can *see* these things; we need no other information in order
to conclude that, despite her many good qualities, Emma is
behaving foolishly. The fact that the narrative voice does not
condemn her forthrightly — that is, merely presents her
actions dramatically — is the source of one level of irony. It
is an irony of understatement, an irony of omission. And
then, when the narrative voice on occasion becomes indistinguishable from Emma's own, we experience another level of
irony — that is, an irony of commission. The partial
coincidence of the two voices — Emma's and the narrator's —
creates a further irony which is an irony of presentation,
since we know *a priori,* despite this coincidence, that Emma
has been acting foolishly. And we know this, once again
paradoxically, because our knowledge as readers is virtually
identical, throughout most of the novel, with the narrator's.
Emma's knowledge of her own actions and their meanings is

not complete; the narrator's knowledge of them, and thus ours, is. Here is a classic example of dramatic irony. The language calls attention to the fact that there are two minds in operation simultaneously, but the mind within the mind of the narrator — that is, Emma's mind — is unaware of this doubleness. Thus when the first mode of irony (that of the narrator's expressionless presentation of Emma's errors) is destroyed by the second mode of irony (the identification of Emma's voice with the narrator's), we as readers still are able to judge Emma accurately because of the previous establishment in our minds, through the narrator's ironic knowledge, of Emma's folly.

Emma's first meditation occurs just after the carriage-ride home from the Westons, during which she has undergone a rather unsettling scene with Mr. Elton, the fashionable clergyman. He has been paying court at Hartfield, and Emma has been assuming all along that his attentions are aimed at her friend Harriet Smith, a penniless and stupid but good-hearted girl of unknown parentage whom Emma has adopted as a companion. In her loneliness and boredom at home with her hypochondriacal father, Emma's two major sources of amusement are instructing Harriet in the ways of "society" and matchmaking. These amusements eventually turn out to be destructive, especially when combined. Emma, through pride and snobbery, succeeds in giving Harriet a false sense of her position in society, arguing that Harriet, as the ward of Miss Emma Woodhouse of Hartfield, could and should make a brilliant marriage. Emma succeeds in breaking off a proposed alliance between Harriet and Robert Martin, a fairly prosperous farmer of or possibly above Harriet's own social rank, and leads her to believe — primarily because Emma wishes it to be true — that the fastidious Mr. Elton is in love with Harriet herself. Mr. Elton, of course, has set his sights on the heiress of Hartfield and proposes marriage to Emma one evening while riding with her in a carriage after a dinner-party at the Westons. Emma is indignant with Mr. Elton on two counts: first, because he should presume to propose to *her*, so much above him in rank; and second, because Emma has assumed all along (and has made Harriet assume as well) that the graces and airs she has been at pains to teach her protegée must have made Mr. Elton fall in love with Harriet. Mr. Elton, who is himself a man of at least respectable origin, is incensed in his turn not only at Emma's brusque refusal to marry him, but even more so at the revelation that Emma considers him a suitable match for Harriet Smith. As he says: "Everybody has their level, but as for myself, I am not, I think, quite so much at a loss. I need not so totally despair of an equal alliance as to be addressing myself to Miss Smith!"[17] Emma has decided that the mere facts of her guardianship of Harriet and Harriet's entrée at Hartfield will make Harriet a desirable match. She does not see that she has been using Harriet, using her as a pawn, as a proxy, as an extension of her own ego, as a way, in short, of avoiding the need to commit herself to marriage and to society. Harriet, after all, has nothing but her own sweet temper to recommend her to any suitor. Mr. Elton, far from thinking Harriet a suitable companion, sees no advantage in an alliance with a young lady of obscure origin, no property, and bovine intellect. Although he later marries a far more stupid woman, though one with some property, at this juncture our sympathies are at least partially with him — we want to see Emma's blind pride and egoism deflated a little. This, indeed, is the effect of the scene on the heroine, who goes home to mull it all over: "The hair was curled and the maid sent away, and Emma sat down to think and be miserable." Following this sentence comes a series of retrospective meditations, connected by a common theme.

Such an overthrow of everything she had been wishing for! Such a development of everything most unwelcome! Such a blow for Harriet! That was the worst of all. Every part of it brought pain and humiliation of some sort or other; but compared with the evil to Harriet, all was light; and she would gladly have submitted to feel yet more mistaken, more in error, more disgraced by misjudgment than she actually was could the effects of her blunders have been confined to herself . . . . How could she have been so deceived! He protested that he had never thought seriously of Harriet — never! She looked back as well as she could, but it was all confusion. She had taken up the idea, she supposed, and made everything bend to it. His manners, however, must have been unmarked, wavering, dubious, or she could not have been so misled.

The picture! How eager he had been about the picture! And the charade! And an hundred other circumstances — how clearly they had seemed to point at Harriet! To be sure, the charade, with its 'ready wit' — but then, the 'soft eyes' — in fact it suited neither; it was a jumble without taste or truth. Who could have seen through such thick-headed nonsense?

* * * * * * *

Certainly she had often, especially of late, thought his manners to herself unnecessarily gallant; but it had passed as his way, as a mere error of judgment, of knowledge, of taste, as one proof, among others, that he had not always lived in the best society; that with all the gentleness of his address, true elegance was sometimes wanting; but till this very day she had never for an instant suspected it to mean anything but grateful respect to her as Harriet's friend.

* * * * * * *

But that he should talk of encouragement, should consider her as aware of his views, accepting his attentions, meaning, in short, to marry him! — should suppose himself her equal in connexion or mind! — look down upon her friend, so well understanding the gradations of rank below him, and be so blind to what rose above as to fancy himself showing no presumption in addressing her! — it was most provoking.

* * * * * * *

But he had fancied her in love with him; that evidently must have been his dependence; and after raving a little about the seeming incongruity of gentle manners and a conceited head, Emma was obliged, in common honesty, to stop and admit that her own behaviour to him had been so complaisant and obliging, so full of courtesy and attention, as (supposing her real motive unperceived) might warrant a man of ordinary observation and delicacy, like Mr. Elton, in fancying himself a very decided favourite. If *she* had so misinterpreted his feelings, she had little right to wonder that *he,* with self-interest to blind him, should have mistaken hers.

The first error, and the worst, lay at her door. It was foolish, it was wrong, to take so active a part in bringing any two people together. It was adventuring too far, assuming too much, making light of what ought to be serious — a trick of what ought to be simple. She was quite concerned and ashamed, and resolved to do such things no more.

* * * * * * *

The distressing explanation she had to make to Harriet and all that poor Harriet would be suffering, with the awkwardness of future meetings, the difficulties of continuing or discontinuing the acquaintance, of subduing feelings, concealing resentment, and avoiding éclat, were enough to occupy her in most unmirthful reflections some time longer, and she went to bed at last with nothing settled but the conviction of her having blundered most dreadfully.[18]

Jane Austen seems to be attempting, in some of these

passages, to give the reader some general sense of the psychic rhythms of an imaginary mind. It is difficult, of course, for language to reproduce exactly the phenomena of consciousness; language may have the capacity to become identical with consciousness, but in fact consciousness races too far ahead of language, and it is virtually impossible for the latter to catch up. While we are thinking of one thing we are also thinking, perhaps at a different level of consciousness, about something else, or perhaps at least starting to do so. Language cannot reproduce this phenomenon precisely; it can, however, suggest the concomitant confusion of mental processes, as in the last forty pages of *Ulysses* and, more specifically, in the first section of the meditation quoted above.

Emma, for the first time in the novel, begins to realize her conceit and folly, and this realization brings on this first meditation (I have quoted here only a fraction of it). Jane Austen lets some idea of Emma's confusion come through to the reader in the first section of the meditation by allowing the voice of her narrator and that of her protagonist to become indistinguishable in places. The first paragraph of the opening section, despite the exclamations, is at least partially omniscient description; one easily detects the narrator's voice in the occurrence several times of the pronoun "she". And yet the thoughts being described are obviously Emma's and not the narrator's, and thus the words he uses inevitably are shaped at least in part by the content of her mind. In the second paragraph the narrative presence is even more difficult to locate. The narrator's relative transparency allows the reader to hear Emma more directly. This section of Emma's meditation emphasizes the "pain" and "humiliation" of her exchange with Mr. Elton, and the confusion of her retrospective feelings about the relationships, both real and imagined, between Mr. Elton and Harriet on the one hand and Mr. Elton and Emma herself on the other. Emma admits that she has been confused and deceived, wonders how such a thing as self-deception could be a part of her nature, suggests to herself in answer that perhaps she has simply made everything "bend" to her own "idea", but concludes that it all cannot be entirely her fault, as Mr. Elton's "manners" must have "misled" her. She is repentant but, as yet, still deceived. She knows she has made a mistake, but she has not as yet discovered why.

The second section of the meditation is all one sentence, and a periodic one at that, but it is not as ambiguous as the preceding passage as far as narrative perspective is concerned. For the narrator is more patently back with us once again, summarizing in omniscient description the thoughts of the protagonist ("she had often", "she had never", and so forth). The third section of the meditation, though once again one sentence, is somewhat more ambiguous. The exclamations suggest that the sentiments are Emma's rather than the narrator's, but the pronoun used throughout is "her". In these passages Emma continues to reprimand herself (not terribly harshly) for misjudging Mr. Elton; she still has little sense of the depth of her blindness.

In the last two sections of the meditation the narrator is again more firmly in control of the language; the narration is in the third person and the past tense, and the words seem more a part of omniscient summary than of any attempt on the narrator's part to reproduce the words Emma is actually thinking. The last section is also one long sentence, and anyone familiar with Jane Austen's characteristic style — epigrammatical, often terse, never flabby, frequently ironic — may well find the style of these meditations rather striking in its complexity. The narrator, though again in control of the language for the most part, nevertheless seems to be influenced in his language and syntax by the texture of the thoughts he is describing to the reader, and thus while the voice we hear is presumably that of the narrator, it is also clear that he is reporting to us the thoughts of Emma as he perceives them — using his mind, that is, as a sort of reflector of hers, thus bringing the two minds into at least a partial coincidence and causing the peculiar kind of irony I have been describing as so radical an element of *Emma*. In these last two sections of the meditation, Emma begins to understand a little more fully that her own behavior has been at fault, and sees, if only for a short time, how "foolish" and "wrong" it is to interfere in other people's lives. "Concerned" and "ashamed", she resolves not to make the same mistake again; and while she does go on in the novel making the same mistake, the mere recognition of error, however transitory that recognition may be, is a step toward that moral vision the acquisition of which is the most important theme of the story. The meditation, appropriately enough, ends emphatically with Emma's discovery of having "blundered".

Emma, like Elizabeth, suffers a crisis of mind in this scene; like Elizabeth, she is irrational and subjective, but like her also she remains logical and articulate in her crisis. She perceives inaccurately due to her self-absorption, but we never doubt her basic intelligence or the possibility that it will eventually enable her to see her errors. One of the things that leads us to this conclusion is the language itself, which once again remains literal, general, and abstract, despite Emma's stress and anxiety. Beneath Emma's confused consciousness, in other words, we are always able to sense the control represented by the narrator's logical and literal mind, expressing itself in the ubiquitously abstract and general phrases we have come to expect from Jane Austen, even when she is describing a psychic convulsion.

The meditation just examined, like the meditation in *Pride and Prejudice*, must be considered one of the pivotal passages of the novel. In it Emma doubts herself for the first (though not the last) time. She begins to see, just a little, that the matchmaking game she has been playing is destructive and dangerous, and that she herself has used faulty judgment. The recognition of limitation, of the egoism of subjectivity, is the recognition of Emma Woodhouse as well as Elizabeth Bennett. Emma begins to realize for the first time that her own conceit and misjudgment are leading her astray. She goes back to her usual ways when the scene ends and the story continues, but nevertheless she has had her first flash of insight, of self-discovery, and thus it is clear that her education is beginning. By the time of the second and climactic meditation in *Emma*, to which the scene just examined is a prelude or companion-piece, Emma's education, her advance from constricting subjectivity to objective self-awareness, has been almost completed. She has been virtually purged of her egotistical pursuits and sees herself, in a final revelation, as she really is. This new knowledge leads, once again, to more accurate perception of others.

Emma, after the Elton debacle, sets her sights on Frank Churchill (who is secretly engaged to Jane Fairfax), first thinking that she might be able to fall in love with him herself, later deciding she could not, and finally once again pushing Harriet to the fore. Churchill's secret engagement necessitates, as a sort of red herring, his ostentatious courting of Emma: he is interested in no one beyond Miss Fairfax, and even if he were not engaged he is a young man sufficiently well-born and wealthy (or soon to be) to eschew an alliance with anyone like poor Harriet Smith. Nevertheless, the indefatigable Emma resolves on a match between Harriet and Churchill, and her various intrigues with him as their object, first for her own benefit and later for Harriet's, form the second movement of the story, the longest series of episodes among the three distinct sections of the novel (Elton, Churchill, Knightley). When Churchill's engagement to Jane is revealed near the end of the story, Emma is once again mortified, repentant, and anxious for Harriet's peace of mind, which Emma herself has unwittingly done the most to disturb. Yet it appears that Harriet, who was heartbroken at Mr. Elton's defection, is not very much disappointed about Frank Churchill's engagement. She has fallen in love instead (and, because of a misunderstanding, with what she thought was Emma's sanction and encouragement) with Mr. Knightley. When Emma learns this, and also that Harriet feels her love for Mr. Knightley is reciprocated, she undergoes a dramatic mental convulsion, seeing herself clearly, in total revelation, for the first time. This final meditation occurs deep in the third volume of the novel.

Emma's eyes were instantly withdrawn; and she sat silently meditating in a fixed attitude for a few minutes. A few minutes were sufficient for making her acquainted with her own heart. A mind like hers, once opening to suspicion, made rapid progress; she touched, she admitted, she acknowledged, the whole truth. Why was it so much worse that Harriet should be in love with Mr. Knightley than with Frank Churchill? Why was the evil so dreadfully increased by Harriet's having some hope of return? It darted through her with the speed of an arrow that Mr. Knightley must marry no one but herself!

Her own conduct, as well as her own heart, was before her in the same few minutes. She saw it all with a clearness which had never blessed her before. How improperly had she been acting by Harriet! How inconsiderate, how indelicate, how irrational, how unfeeling, had been her conduct! What blindness, what madness, had led her on! It struck her with dreadful force, and she was ready to give it every bad name in the world. Some portion of respect for herself, however, in spite of all these demerits, some concern for her own appearance, and a strong sense of justice by Harriet (there would be no need of *compassion* to the girl who believed herself loved by Mr. Knightley — but justice required that she should not be made unhappy by any coldness now) gave Emma the resolution to sit and endure further with calmness, with even apparent kindness.

*   *   *   *   *   *   *

The rest of the day, the following night, were hardly enough for her thoughts. She was bewildered amidst the confusion of all that had rushed on her within the last few hours. Every moment had brought a fresh surprise; and every surprise must be a matter of humiliation to her. How to understand it all! How to understand the deceptions she had been thus practicing on herself and living under! The blunders, the blindness of her own head and heart! She sat still, she walked about, she tried her own room, she tried the shrubbery — in every place, every posture, she perceived that she had acted most weakly; that she had been imposed on by others in a most mortifying degree; that she had been imposing on herself in a degree yet more mortifying; that she was wretched and should probably find this day but the beginning of wretchedness.

*   *   *   *   *   *   *

How long had Mr. Knightley been so dear to her, as every feeling declared him now to be?(1) When had his influence, such influence, begun? (2) When had he succeeded to that place in her affection which Frank Churchill had once, for a short period, occupied? (3) She looked back; she compared the two — compared them, as they had always stood in her estimation, from the time of the latter's becoming known to her — and as they must at any time have been compared by her had it — oh! had it, by any blessed felicity — occurred to her to institute the comparison. (4) She saw that there never had been a time when she did not consider Mr. Knightley as infinitely the superior or when his regard for her had not been infinitely the most dear. (5) She saw that in persuading herself, in fancying, in acting to the contrary, she had been entirely under a delusion, totally ignorant of her own heart — and, in short, that she had never really cared for Frank Churchill at all!(6)

*   *   *   *   *   *   *

This was the conclusion of the first series of reflections. This was the knowledge of herself, on the first question of inquiry, which she reached; and without being long in reaching it. She was most sorrowfully indignant, ashamed of every sensation but the one revealed to her — her affection for Mr. Knightley. Every other part of her mind was disgusting.

With insufferable vanity had she believed herself in the secret of everybody's feelings, with unpardonable arrogance proposed to arrange everybody's destiny. She was proved to have been universally mistaken, and she had not quite done nothing — for she had done mischief.

*   *   *   *   *   *   *

Mr. Knightley and Harriet Smith! It was a union to distance every wonder of the kind. The attachment of Frank Churchill and Jane Fairfax became commonplace, threadbare, stale in the comparison, exciting no surprise, presenting no disparity, affording nothing to be said or thought. Mr. Knightley and Harriet Smith! Such an elevation on her side! Such a debasement on his! . . . . Could it be? No, it was impossible. And yet it was very far, very far, from impossible. Was it a new circumstance for a man of first-rate abilities to be captivated by very inferior powers? Was it new for one, perhaps too busy to seek, to be the prize of a girl who would seek him? Was it new for anything in this world to be unequal, inconsistent, incongruous — for chance and circumstance (as second causes) to direct the human fate?

Oh! Had she never brought Harriet forward! Had she left her where she ought and where he had told her she ought! Had she not, with a folly which no tongue could express, prevented her marrying the unexceptionable young man who would have made her happy and respectable in the line of life to which she ought to belong, all would have been safe; none of this dreadful sequel would have been.

How Harriet could ever have had the presumption to raise her thoughts to Mr. Knightley! How she could dare to fancy herself the chosen of such a man till actually assured of it! But Harriet was less humble, had fewer scruples than formerly. Her inferiority, whether of mind or situation, seemed little felt. She had seemed more sensible of Mr. Elton's being to stoop in marrying her than she now seemed of Mr. Knightley's. Alas! Was not that her own doing too! Who had been at pains to give Harriet notions of self-consequence but herself? Who but herself had taught her that she was to elevate herself if possible, and that her claims were great to a high worldly establishment? If Harriet, from being humble, were grown vain, it was her doing too.

*   *   *   *   *   *   *

Till now that she was threatened with its loss, Emma had never known how much of her happiness depended on being *first* with Mr. Knightley, first in interest and affection. Satisfied that it was so, and feeling it her due, she had enjoyed it without reflection, and only in the dread of being supplanted found how inexpressibly important it had been. Long, very long, she felt she had been first . . . . Harriet Smith might think herself not unworthy of being peculiarly, exclusively, passionately loved by Mr. Knightley. *She* could not. She could not flatter herself with any idea of blindness in his attachment to *her*. She had received a very recent proof of its impartiality. How shocked had he been by her behaviour to Miss Bates! How directly, how strongly, had he expressed himself to her on the subject! Not too strongly for the offence — but far, far too strongly to issue from any feeling softer than upright justice and clear-sighted goodwill. She had no hope, nothing to deserve the name of hope, that he could have that sort of affection for herself which was now in question; but there was a hope (at times a slight one, at times much stronger) that Harriet might have deceived herself and be overrating his regard for *her*. Wish it she must 19

Emma is actually referred to as "meditating" in the first of the passages quoted, and this is a series of meditations in which she finally realizes her true feelings and thus the vanity and error of her former pursuits. In the first part of the meditation she arrives immediately at the true state of her feelings and finally understands that she has loved Mr. Knightley all along.

The first section is in large measure omniscient description. The narrator, using the third person and the past tense for the most part, describes Emma's thoughts as he perceives them, including the sentence that represents the central moment of the meditation: "It darted through her with the speed of an arrow that Mr. Knightley must marry no one but herself!" And yet the questions in the first paragraph and the exclamations in the second paragraph of this section indicate that the language is not wholly the narrator's. The questions and exclamations are presumably Emma's — that is, they represent the probable rhythm of her thoughts. Thus once again the narrator's mind seems to be acting as a sort of transparent container of Emma's, and the resulting language is an ironic product of this relationship. The second section of the meditation is similar in construction. The narrator's past-tense, third-person summary is couched in the exclamatory terms Emma is presumably using to herself. The third section of the meditation begins with a series of questions Emma asks herself. Parts of this section are surely reminiscent in many ways of parts of Elizabeth Bennet's meditation. Sentences five and six of this section begin with the phrase "She saw", just as in the meditation in *Pride and Prejudice* Elizabeth is depicted as motionlessly seeing, remembering, realizing what she had been ignorant of previously, and so on. Here, Emma finally "sees" into her own heart, just as Elizabeth Bennet "sees" into the nature of her prejudice against Darcy. And "seeing" is all that does occur in this section of the meditation; nothing external *happens*, but the heroine, through self-exploration, arrives at new knowledge about herself as a result of her new insight into the real nature of her relationship with another. Emma will then, later on, become a more perceptive and sympathetic member of her immediate society. Once again, it is the new perspective on a man that provides the beginning of self-knowledge for the woman.

In the fourth section Emma's meditation is called a "series of reflections", the product of which is new "knowledge of herself". As a result of meditation, of self-exploration, her own "vanity" and "arrogance" have been "revealed" to her. What is implicit here once again is the movement from the egoism of self-absorption to the objective knowledge which is the fruit of self-discovery. Emma's pride and her tendency to subjectify everything dissolve for the most part with the commencement of this new self-awareness. Elizabeth Bennet underwent the same process.

Vestiges of Emma's characteristic vanity are still apparent at the beginning of the fifth section but have disappeared almost completely by the end of it. This fifth section, combined with the third, forms the core of Emma's second and climactic meditation, the climax of a movement away from excessive subjectivity and egoism and toward objectivity of perception and sympathy. Emma sees that she has transferred part of her wordly vanity from herself to Harriet, and that this may spell unhappiness for them both. She finally, and quite rightly, blames herself for everything. The language in this section, however, becomes more ambiguous once again. The first paragraph and the first half of the last paragraph of this part of the meditation are couched in sentiments that are undoubtedly Emma's own; the narrator once again has become more transparent in order to let them come through to the reader more directly: "Mr. Knightley and Harriet Smith! Such an elevation on her side! Such a debasement on his! . . . . Could it be?" These are presumably Emma's thoughts, but the question of who is actually giving voice to them once again is not easily answered. Either the narrator is giving us his own view of what Emma is thinking, or she is speaking directly to us, or they are speaking together in some combination with one voice — the answer cannot be known for sure. This particular series of passages thus also exemplifies the occasionally double irony of the language. On the one hand there is the irony of Emma's folly, a folly which she is just now discovering and which we and the narrator have known about all along. Beneath this level of dramatic irony there is what I have called the irony of presentation: the narrator and the character seem throughout much of this passage to be indistinguishable, and yet it is the essential detachment and objectivity of the narrator in earlier sections of the novel that have enabled us to read Emma correctly in the first place. The convergence, at this climactic moment, of the narrator's point of view and Emma's provides a final, ubiquitous irony. Emma's revelation has its genesis in the fact that her knowledge has finally caught up with the narrator's, just as in a first-person novel the protagonist often reaches the point at the end of the novel where his older self — that is, the narrator — began in the novel's opening pages. Emma has discovered what the narrator has known all along, and thus this final revelation is also a final moment of dramatic irony.

The sixth and final section of this meditation returns for the most part to omniscient description. For what is undeniably the first time in the novel, Emma in this final section underestimates herself. The discovery of her own vanity and blindness has led her one step toward humility, genuine humility, and she now mistakenly assumes that Mr. Knightley could not possibly love her. She has come a long way from her high-handed rejection of Mr. Elton.

Emma is being educated. Her mind seems to be working somewhat more rationally at the end of the novel than at the beginning. In early chapters her mind was turned in upon herself most of the time, and thus in her excessive subjectivity she failed to see how selfishly and foolishly she was behaving. The subject of her thoughts was usually herself or her own desires, and if not these then other people only as they related to herself. Harriet, for example, was important to her merely as an extension of her own ego. But like Elizabeth Bennet, Emma finally sees into the nature of her blindness, and her mind then begins to turn outward. She too comprehends her own folly; her reasoning faculties seem to become more acute as the novel progresses, until finally, at the end of the novel, she sees herself in total revelation and is thus able to begin cultivating more assiduously the virtues of selflessness and rationality. For her, as for Elizabeth Bennet, self-revelation thus leads to an increased objectivity of perception. Always intelligent and articulate, even during a crisis of mind, Emma emerges from the concentrated mental stress at the end of the novel a more perceptive and sympathetic person.

But the mind of the heroine, to which I have paid so much attention in this discussion, is after all, one must always remember, only a mind within a mind. The narrative voice is almost always present, however tenuously; there seems to be a constant copresence of two minds in this novel, that of the heroine and that of the narrator, always superior in judgment and knowledge to the heroine. The narrator, in spite of his sympathetic following of Emma's mental processes, nevertheless knows how the story is going to come out; while the heroine is thinking, the reader is constantly aware, because of the narrator's total access to the mind he is describing and his use of the past tense and the third person in formulating that description, that the protagonist is thinking within the context of a surrounding mind, the mind of the narrator. The narrator's language, in other words, is posterior to the consciousness of the character. This, as I have suggested, provides for an almost continuous source of irony throughout the novel.

Readers of Jane Austen's novels have of course long considered her fiction "ironic" in some vague way. The adjective is used constantly, often without any clear understanding of how complex are its operations in the novels. Verbal irony — that is, saying one thing and meaning something else — is a common form, a form often recognized by Jane Austen's readers with little difficulty. The dramatic irony in Jane Austen's novels, which results from the reader's knowing at some times more than the character — a knowledge due to the omniscient knowledge of the narrator, when the narrator chooses to express that superior knowledge — is once again a convention we find ourselves familiar and easy with. But Jane Austen's irony, as I have been suggesting, at times reaches a third stratum, a stratum resulting from the narrative texture of her novels. This third level of irony is an irony of omission, or perhaps rather of withdrawal, and occurs when the narrative voice *stops* emanating from a position posterior to the consciousness of the character and instead becomes muffled by the thinking voice of the fictive personality. Such a withdrawal, because of our knowledge that the narrator understands the situation better than the character (as he does in *Emma*), creates this additional level of irony, an irony that exists in permitting the deluded protagonist to express her inaccurate impressions in unison with the narrative voice, when in fact both the reader and the narrator know that her impressions are not accurate. In failing to continue to say so, the narrator causes what I have called an irony of withdrawal. Thus Jane Austen's irony is no simple matter; it is inevitably connected with and dependent upon the narrative structuring of her novels, a structuring which is itself a complex, one might say a baroque, affair.

One may well ask why Jane Austen chooses to adopt this complex method of narration. I think the answer is clear. What is at issue in most of her novels — and most dramatically in *Emma*, as we have seen — is her protagonist's self-delusion in relation to judgment of others. The reader, encountering a narrative voice emanating from varying distances between himself and the protagonist, constantly finds this central problem of *perspective* laid in his path. Who is speaking, and from what vantage-point? How veracious is the voice we hear, and what components might it contain? These elements of ironic confusion invite us to raise such questions as I am raising here, questions relating above all to perspective, perception, and intuitive comprehension. These are the issues being convulsively faced by Jane Austen's protagonists, and thus it seems logical that her narrative structuring should raise them for the reader as well.

It also seems logical that it should raise them in language that remains consistently, as I have been suggesting, literal, general, and abstract. Certainly these qualities of Jane Austen's language tell us, among other things, that while the protagonist may be having difficulty developing a coherent view of herself and of the world, the omniscient mind which surrounds the protagonist has no difficulty in doing so, and is only waiting, as it were, for the protagonist's understanding to catch up with its own. *Emma*, like *Pride and Prejudice*, begins with a general statement: "Emma Woodhouse, handsome, clever, and rich, with a comfortable home and happy disposition, seemed to unite some of the best blessings of existence, and had lived nearly twenty-one years in the world with very little to distress or vex her." Even in these meditation scenes, with all their storm and stress, the language remains literal and abstract, reminding us that one of the things the protagonist has been lacking is a self-disciplined perspective upon herself and the rest of the world as well.

III

The meditation scenes in *Emma*, like the ones examined in *Pride and Prejudice*, are pivotal scenes in the novel's thematic progression. In both novels the meditation scenes, in which the heroine ultimately views the novel's hero as well as herself in a new light, function primarily as vehicles for self-revelation. Darcy is not a static character by any means, yet he changes much less than Elizabeth does; Mr. Knightley does not change at all. In both cases the novel's heroine undergoes a spiritual convulsion of sorts and regards the man with whom she is paired in the light of her own new knowledge — a knowledge of herself.

In the meditation scenes in both of these novels by Jane Austen the heroines become enlightened on the subject of their own egoism. Certainly both Elizabeth and Emma begin as egoists imprisoned within their own subjectivity and move from this visionless realm to one of self-knowledge and objective sympathy. The crux of such movement occurs principally in these central meditation scenes. Jane Austen seems to feel that a complete knowledge of one's self is a prerequisite for the dissipation of blinding subjectivity in relation to judgment of others. Elinor and Marianne in *Sense and Sensibility*, Fanny in *Manfield Park*, Catherine in *Northanger Abbey*, and Anne in *Persuasion* — as well as a host of supporting characters in all of Jane Austen's novels — are egoists of sorts. Yet none of the protagonists in the other novels indulges in such an elaborate phalanx of retrospective meditations as do Elizabeth and Emma.

Yet even during these moments of psychic convulsion, as I have suggested, the minds of Jane Austen's heroines seem to work logically. The rhythms of their mental processes seem a bit nervous and abrupt during these mental crises, punctuated as they are by sentence fragments, exclamations, and self-questioning. Yet the heroines seem to remain, for the most part, articulate and logical; their thoughts are usually expressed in terms of balanced antitheses, clearly, forcefully, and even at times with rhetorical elegance. And yet they both make mistakes. With all the evidence before them that is necessary to arrive at a true evaluation of people and of the true state of things, both Elizabeth and Emma manage, because of their egoism, to assemble their evidential data erroneously. For Jane Austen the relative perceptivity of the human mind seems to depend a great deal on the amount of self-knowledge possessed by the person attempting to perceive. Those who are excessively subjective and thus self-deluded tend to mistake other people and things as well as themselves — perhaps because they do not understand themselves sufficiently. Self-knowledge brings with it more objective perception and thus an increase in the rationality and objective comprehension of the mind itself. One must look in to see out.

For Jane Austen, then, there must be some sort of epistemological interchange in the educational process. One's view of the world is colored in large measure by one's view of one's self; and by the same token, one cannot view one's self clearly if one does not see accurately what is outside of one's self. The two things are interdependent; self-deception in relation to others, which is Jane Austen's paramount theme, inevitably includes a mistaken reading both of self and of others. The two parts of this equation are virtually inseparable. The ideal is to see the self and others — and the relationship between them — clearly. Subject and object are equally important, and even determine each other to some extent. The individual usually is capable of seeing the rest of the world only in the shadow of his own egoism; and he is equally capable of seeing himself in terms of a false shadow imposed from without, based on his partial view of the rest of the world. The imagination, then, is something to be subordinated to empirical data. Elizabeth and Emma imagine both themselves and others to be other than they really are, and it is only when their imaginations are conquered by truth — truth literal, general, and abstract — that any epistemological interchange can take place easily. Jane Austen would not argue for the repression of the imagination, but she would argue for its subordination to logic. In this she once again unmistakably demonstrates her eighteenth-century roots. One of the obvious morals of *Emma* is that truth, sincerity, and clarity are infinitely more valuable than the deception and obfuscation attendant upon an inordinately active imagination — though they are sometimes less interesting. When this fact finally comes home to Emma, she has not only learned where the imaginative capacities belong on any scale of personal attributes — she has also learned that they are aesthetically less satisfying and complete than the truth of rational logic. This, too, is part of her education in values, and part of Jane Austen's lesson.

When one looks at Jane Austen's literary heirs he sees that many of them adopted similar techniques and objectives and added one other ingredient to the language in scenes in which indirect interior monologues occur, an ingredient that is distinctly missing in the central passages I have examined in *Pride and Prejudice* and *Emma:* metaphor.[20]

[1] See Professor Mudrick's *Jane Austen: Irony as Defense and Discovery* (1952). Lionel Trilling, in an essay on *Mansfield Park* in *The Opposing Self* (1955), indirectly attacks Mudrick's position and makes a point, somewhat tersely, similar to the one I am making here in connection with a different novel.

[2] Not until Volume II, Chapter XIII of the novel. Some editions of Jane Austen's novels number the chapters consecutively and some follow the original divisions into volumes. In this chapter all references to Jane Austen's novels are to the standard edition, *The Novels of Jane Austen*, sometimes called the Oxford Illustrated Jane Austen, ed. R.W. Chapman, 6 vols., London (1923), revised in subsequent editions. I am using the third edition, published in 1932. The text in this edition is based on a collation of earlier editions and includes minor works, notes, indexes, and illustrations from contemporary sources. *Pride and Prejudice* is Volume II of this edition.

[3] See Booth's *The Rhetoric of Fiction* (1961), especially chapters VII-IX, pp. 169-266, *passim.*

[4] This has often been noticed by critics. See, for example, Dorothy Van Ghent's essay on *Pride and Prejudice* in *The English Novel: Form and Function* (1953); Howard Babb, *Jane Austen's Novels: The Fabric of Dialogue* (1962); and Mary Lascelles, *Jane Austen and Her Art* (1939).

[5]Babb makes several of these same points.

[6]A.W. Litz (see Chapter 1, n.4) and Mary Lascelles also hint at this.

[7]I use the phrase "indirect interior monologue" to distinguish it from direct interior monologue, in which there is no authorial interference of any kind. Indirect interior monologue is more like omniscient description or indirect discourse, in which the presence of the mediating narrative voice is continuously felt. In helping to clarify these matters in my own mind, I am indebted to Robert Humphrey's *Stream of Consciousness in the Modern Novel* (1954).

[8]See Wilson's monumental essay, "Dickens: The Two Scrooges," in *The Wound and the Bow* (1947), pp. 1-85.

[9]Litz also mentions such a progression in passing, but does not develop any extended discussion of the matter.

[10]Volume II, Chapter XIII, pp. 205-208, *passim*. Between the first two sections of the meditation I have omitted a paragraph in which Elizabeth reviews her own mental image of Wickham, weighs it against Darcy's account of him, and begins at last to doubt the former gentleman. Between sections two and three I have left out only a few sentences, in which the course of Elizabeth's revelation continues apace: "How differently did everything now appear in which [Wickham] was concerned!" Between sections three and four I have omitted nothing.

[11]The novel's originally projected title, as a matter of fact, was *First Impressions*.

[12]Litz also makes some of these points in his excellent discussion of the novel.

[13]See n.1, above.

[14]See Forster's *Aspects of the Novel* (1927), Chapter Four, pp. 65-82.

[15]Professor Mudrick's opinion is that Emma, like Jane Austen herself, simply lacks "tenderness". I think, however, that Mr. Mudrick's rather dour view of Jane Austen's personality has interfered considerably with his assessment of the novel. Emma is certainly "tender" with her father and Mrs. Weston, and deeply regrets her earlier treatment of Miss Bates and Jane Fairfax. And doubtlessly by the end of the novel, when she realizes her love for Mr. Knightley, her capacity for "tenderness" is unmistakably demonstrated once again.

[16]Wayne Booth, in *The Rhetoric of Fiction*, hints at a source of irony in *Emma* being the copresence of a third-person, unreliable, dramatized narrator — Emma herself — and a reliable, dramatized narrator: Jane Austen, the implied author. Yet he does not pursue this subject at any great length in order more closely to examine, as I do shortly, the additional stratum of irony created by the complexity of narrative structure in the novel.

[17]Volume I, Chapter XV, p.132. *Emma* is the fourth volume in Chapman's edition.

[18]Volume I, Chapter XVI, pp. 134-137, *passim*. Between the first two sections of the meditation quoted in the text I have left nothing out; the division between the passages was made to facilitate analysis. Between sections two and three I have omitted two paragraphs in which Emma recalls Mr. Knightley's warnings to her that Mr. Elton "would never marry indiscreetly," but goes on to decide that Mr. Elton's proposal to her nevertheless has "sunk him in her opinion." Between sections three and four I have left out several sentences in which Emma reassures herself, by dwelling on the differences in rank between them, that she was right to refuse Mr. Elton. And between the fourth and fifth sections I have

omitted a paragraph in which Emma blames herself for the inevitable disappointment to be suffered by Harriet, and yet also makes it clear to the reader that she
has not finished meddling with her friend's matrimonial prospects (" '. . . oh, no, I
could not endure William Cox — a pert young lawyer' ").

[19] Volume III, Chapters XI-XII, pp. 407-416, *passim.* Between the first two
sections of this meditation I have omitted several paragraphs in which Emma en-
courages Harriet to tell her what grounds she (Harriet) has for assuming that Mr.
Knightley returns her love for him. Harriet's story sounds very convincing to
Emma, who admits to herself that Harriet has "done nothing to forfeit [her]
regard and interest," but also wishes that she "had never seen her!" Between
sections two and three I have left out two sentences in which Emma says to
herself that she must try "thoroughly" to "understand . . . her own heart."
Between the third and fourth sections I have omitted nothing; the division
between the passages was made to facilitate analysis. Between sections four and
five I have left out two sentences in which Emma lays all the blame for the
predicament she is in upon herself. And between the last two sections of the
meditation I have once again omitted nothing; a division was made here, however,
primarily because the eleventh chapter ends with the end of the fifth section and
the twelfth chapter begins at the beginning of the sixth.

[20] In using figurative language so sparingly, Jane Austen was following the taste of
the eighteenth-century writers. The avoidance of tropes became a commonplace
in the eighteenth century, stemming in large measure from the great campaign
waged by the Royal Society during the Restoration in favor of the so-called
"plain" style.

CHAPTER THREE

GEORGE ELIOT (1819 - 1880)

The novels of George Eliot have several things in common
with those of Jane Austen. The subject of manners in English
provincial life of the recent past is the usual subject of both
writers, although Jane Austen deals more consistently than
her successor with her own contemporaries. Like Jane Austen's
novels, George Eliot's usually grow out of the psychology of
her characters. The "plot" of her novels is often that of a
character's mental growth, a central movement surrounded by
a multitude of sub-plots concerned with the mental growth of
more peripheral characters. Like Jane Austen, George Eliot
employs what James calls the "scenic" method; that is to say,
she subscribes to the idea that scenes must be rendered
dramatically and not merely described.[1] Both Jane Austen
and George Eliot prefer to use women as their chief
protagonists, and the "education" of the heroine will be as
radical a theme in the novels of George Eliot as it was in
those by Jane Austen already examined. Both are intensely
"moral" writers — that is, they are occupied fundamentally
with moral behavior, and with manners as a reflection of it.

The prevailing thematic movement in all of George Eliot's
novels, as several critics have pointed out, is the movement
of many of the protagonists away from egoism and toward a
more objective moral vision.[2] Such was the movement of
Elizabeth Bennet and Emma Woodhouse, and such is also the
movement of Dorothea Brooke and Gwendolen Harleth, the
heroines of the two novels by George Eliot examined in this
chapter. George Eliot believed that art has a social, moral
mission — that its twin goals should be the destruction of
egoism and the creation of sympathy for others. Like Dickens
and Dostoevski, to name just two examples among novelists,
she also believed that suffering leads to — is even a prerequisite

51

for — increased understanding and sympathy for one's fellow men (Adam Bede is a prime example). The moral process in her novels is from experience to vision to sympathy, or, to state it another way, from egoism to despair to objectivity. This is the formula B.J. Paris applies to George Eliot's novels, and I think it is an accurate one.[3]

In both *Middlemarch* (1871-72) and *Daniel Deronda* (1876) the paramount theme is the education of the heroine.[4] As in *Pride and Prejudice* and *Emma*, the movement of the heroine from self-absorption to objectivity has its genesis in her suddenly altered perspective upon a male protagonist, a perspective which leads her to self-examination and thence to self-knowledge and greater understanding of those among whom she lives.

George Eliot, Barbara Hardy tells us, saw the novel as a tragic form, and her characters typically have the tragic flaw of egoism.[5] Many of her novels, of course, end happily, and when this is the case it is only after the tragic flaw has in some way been expiated, usually through a painful movement from innocence to experience. Such a movement in George Eliot's novels results from the dissipation of moral blindness and the growth of feeling. The plot and the characters may change from novel to novel, but this element stays the same. Her constant goal was to awaken and enlarge the sympathy and the moral perception of her characters and, through them, of her readers as well.

Ignorance, for George Eliot, is a result of faulty vision, of egoism, while understanding comes from the knowledge of experience, the knowledge of "sympathy". The end of self-absorption is the beginning of experience. It follows quite naturally that George Eliot's novels include many passages relevant in one way or another to *vision*, that is, to the way people see or avoid seeing. As Reva Stump has brilliantly demonstrated, the movement toward or away from moral vision is the movement of almost all of George Eliot's characters.[6] The result of a growth in vision is amelioration of the self through increased understanding of the world. This, George Eliot would hope, would be true of her readers as well as of her characters. She was able to combine a powerful social vision with the expert and sensitive analysis of people's private motives, and thus her novels are usually both chronicles of manners and histories of a soul.

Man must learn to know himself and to live without illusion, else he will never emerge from his prison of egoism — this is a radical theme in George Eliot's novels, and thus it is not surprising to find in them meditation scenes similar to those examined in Chapter Two. In *Pride and Prejudice*, Elizabeth first began to know herself when she discovered how she had misjudged Darcy. In *Emma*, Emma's blindness to her own real nature began to fade a little after her miscalculations regarding Mr. Elton, and disappeared altogether when she discovered the true state of her feelings about Mr. Knightley. In both *Middlemarch* and *Daniel Deronda*, George Eliot's heroine, because of her own egoism, misjudges the man she marries and starts on the road to objective moral vision through the dawning of self-knowledge. These misjudgments do not mean that her protagonists are any less intelligent or articulate than Jane Austen's heroines; rather, as I shall demonstrate, George Eliot's characters differ from them primarily in being residents of a physically determined universe, in failing to see this, and therefore in reasoning from inaccurate premises. They do *not* possess all the evidential data necessary for making correct decisions. Their imaginations, also generated by egoism, propel them to see things that are not really there and to fail to see things that are. George Eliot's physical and psychological determinism is defined at least in part in the dynamic and mechanical metaphors she uses to describe the clash of physical and psychological energies in the world of her novels. In the process of portraying to her readers the peculiar nature of this world, the narrative voice in her novels, which at times follows the psychological convulsions of her heroines with close sympathy, also is capable of detaching itself from the characters it describes for purposes of general commentary, resulting in a continuously fluctuating ironic distance between the narrative presence and the characters in the novel. These things should be evident shortly.

II

*Middlemarch,*George Eliot's greatest novel, deals with English provincial society just before the Reform Bill, and within that society predominantly with the middle class. The various plots of the novel are different versions of the same story — the struggle to achieve human fellowship upon society's moral battlefield.

In *Middlemarch* it is Dorothea's vision of duty that leads her astray. She sees Mr. Casaubon not as he is — a humorless, selfish pedant — but as she would like him to be: Pascal, Oberlin, St. Augustine all rolled into one, a brilliant but misunderstood scholar who needs the selfless care of a devoted wife. In her desire for martyrdom she also misjudges herself, for she is unfit temperamentally to be the wife of such a man. He wants not a wife but an obsequious servant, and he proposes to her because he believes she will be capable of performing as one. Thus there is lack of perception on both sides.[7] Dorothea's recognition of her mistake is gradual and painful, punctuated intermittently by spells of remorse for what she sometimes feels is her unworthiness as a wife. Her final understanding of Mr. Casaubon's nature is the beginning of her realization of her own. In her emancipation from the blindness of her own egoism she finally realizes that her desire for religious justification cannot be fulfilled in the world she is living in, that some of her most ardent needs cannot be satisfied, and that her "mission" in the world is to be a real wife to a real man and a mother to their children. Such a realization is a difficult process, as self-comprehension always is; thus her "education" is gradual. Its most rapid progress occurs in two meditation scenes.

The first of these comes shortly after Dorothea's marriage to Mr. Casaubon, during their "honeymoon" in Rome. Dorothea has learned a good deal about her new husband during their six weeks of marriage, more indeed than she learned about him during their lackluster courtship. She is now beginning to acquire the "art of vision".

Ruins and basilicas, palaces and colossi, set in the midst of a sordid present, where all that was living and warm-blooded seemed sunk in the deep degeneracy of a superstition divorced from reverence; the dimmer but yet eager Titanic life gazing and struggling on walls and ceilings; the long vistas of white forms whose marble eyes seemed to hold the monotonous light of an alien world: all this vast wreck of ambitious ideals, sensuous and spiritual, mixed confusedly with the signs of breathing forgetfulness and degradation, at first jarred her as with an electric shock, and then urged themselves on her with that ache belonging to a glut of confused ideas which check the flow of emotion.

*   *   *   *   *   *   *

Dorothea was crying, and if she had been required to state the cause, she could only have done so in some such general words as I have already used: to have been driven to be more particular would have been like trying to give a history of the light and shadows; for that new real future which was replacing the imaginary drew its material from the endless minutiae by which her view of Mr. Casaubon and her wifely relation, now that she was married to him, was gradually changing with the secret motion of a watch-hand from what it had been in her maiden dream. It was too early yet for her fully to recognize or at least admit the change, still more for her to have readjusted that devotedness which was so necessary a part of her mental life that she was almost sure sooner or later to recover it. Permanent rebellion, the disorder of a life without some loving reverent resolve, was not possible to her; but she was now in an interval when the very force of her nature heightened its confusion.

*   *   *   *   *   *   *

But was not Mr. Casaubon just as learned as before? Had his forms of expression changed, or his sentiments become less laudable? . . . did his chronology fail him, or his ability to state not only a theory but the names of those who held it; or his provision for giving the heads of any subject on demand? And was not Rome the place in the world to give free play to such accomplishments? . . . How was it that in the weeks since her marriage, Dorothea had not distinctly observed but felt with a stifling depression, that the large vistas and wide fresh air which she had dreamed of finding in her husband's mind were replaced by anterooms and winding passages which seemed to lead nowhither?

*   *   *   *   *   *   *

These characteristics, fixed and unchangeable as bone in Mr. Casaubon, might have remained longer unfelt by Dorothea if she had been encouraged to pour forth her girlish and womanly feeling — if he would have held her hands between his and listened with the delight of tenderness and understanding to all the little histories which made up her experience, and would have given her the same sort of intimacy in return, so that the past life of each could be included in their mutual knowledge and affection — or if she could have fed her affection with those childlike caresses which are the bent of every sweet woman, who has begun by showering kisses on the hard pate of her bald doll, creating a happy soul within that woodenness from the wealth of her own love.[8]

The first section of the meditation is one periodic sentence; Dorothea's mental processes are appropriately described by the narrative voice in complex sentence structure. Her "glut of confused ideas" tumble over each other "confusedly" in a series of images, architectural images. This is one of the striking features of the passage.[9] The metaphorical structure, however, exists only for the reader and not for Dorothea herself. That is, the reader is invited to draw a parallel here between the "vast wreck" of Rome's "ambitious ideals"and Dorothea's, between the collapsed edifices of Rome and the collapsing edifice of Dorothea's marriage. There is no evidence in the passage itself, however, that the parallel exists for Dorothea also. Instead, what the final phrase of the passage tells the reader is that Dorothea is subject "to a glut of confused ideas which check the flow of emotion." This in turn suggests that for George Eliot the relation of a character to his environment is an experience that is more properly expressed epistemologically than metaphorically or symbolically. That is to say, Rome does not specifically remind Dorothea of her own ruin; it simply has a shattering effect on her mind. Rome for her is not a symbolical experience but rather an epistemological one; the experience of Rome in itself breaks the sequence of Dorothea's ordinary flow of emotion and makes her that much more vulnerable to the discovery of her own unhappiness.[10] Another pattern of images introduced here and repeated often later on is that of the juxtaposition of light and darkness. The "dimmer" life of the museums is contrasted with the "monotonous light" of Rome, and the reader is told in the sentence immediately following that "forms both pale and flowing took possession of" Dorothea's senses. The light-dark pattern will recur, with more thematic relevance, further on, and also makes its appearance in *Daniel Deronda*.[11]

In the second section of the meditation, the first sentence once again is long, complex, and metaphorical. The language here, as in the first section of the meditation, seems to be primarily that of the novel's omniscient narrative voice, but this very question of whose language it is is openly discussed at this point by the narrative voice in the following terms: "if Dorothea had been required to state the cause [of her suffering] , she could only have done so in some such general words as I have already used". The narrator, using the first person, reminds us that Dorothea's thoughts come through to us in his own voice, but claims that he is justified in speaking for Dorothea because if she had been allowed or able to speak to the reader directly she would have used the same words. The distinction between the narrator and the character, then, is somewhat blurred here, for the narrator claims to be using the same language the character would have used had she been able to speak to the reader directly. We have witnessed the same blurring, the same confusion, in Jane Austen's novels, but in the latter the narrative voice never states the problem for us as directly as George Eliot's narrator does here. Also, the complexities of narrative perspective never become quite as ambiguous in George Eliot's novels, for reasons I shall explain shortly.

The last two sentences of this second section remind the reader that he is dealing with Dorothea's "mental life", and specifically with the "disorder" and "confusion" of it. The disorder and confusion, as the first sentence makes clear, is due to Dorothea's changing assessment of her husband, a changing assessment that is appropriately described in terms of actual images of change. The distinction between light and shadow, for example, must be complex and difficult of definition, and is thus particularly relevant to any preoccupation with the problem of "vision"; this is why the light-shadow image is used to define the gradualness of Dorothea's altering perception. It also foreshadows a more extended use of the metaphor to distinguish between the darkness of past ignorance and the light of new knowledge. The other image, that of Dorothea's view of Mr. Casaubon "gradually changing with the secret motion of a watch-hand", is also appropriate. George Eliot frequently alludes to the minute workings of small mechanisms as a paradigm for interpersonal relations; cause and effect in her world is a complex web of interaction and continuous alteration. Dorothea's relationship to Mr. Casaubon is just now beginning to change, while she herself, though undergoing the process of acquiring a new objectivity of perception, remains at this point basically the same person. Her real alteration begins only with her central revelation later in the novel.[12]

The latter part of this second section also gives the reader some important information about Dorothea's mental makeup. Dorothea, one learns, needs to be devoted to someone or something, to organize her life around "some loving reverent resolve". "Devotedness" is a necessary part of her mental life. She wants religious justification for her life, she thinks that Casaubon embodies it, and this is why she has chosen to devote herself to him. All of these things are asserted. What she wants is not foolish, but it is both impossible and self-blinding — impossible because she lives in a world that cannot satisfy religious needs, blinding because it causes her to misjudge others, specifically in this case her husband. For George Eliot, people have fixed natures, and this is Dorothea's. The balance of the elements of her nature is capable of undergoing rearrangement, but as of now this is simply the way she is. George Eliot's psychological determinism will emerge in even greater relief later on.[13]

George Eliot employs architectural imagery once again in the third section of the meditation. The "vistas" (see n.11) reappear, now beginning to be "replaced by anterooms and winding passages which seemed to lead nowither."[14] Dorothea sees her "vistas" slowly closing, "stifling" her as they do so. It was marriage to Mr. Casaubon's mind, to the expansiveness of his intellect, that had represented to her, along with the desire to serve him, "the large vistas and wide fresh air" she was seeking, and it is precisely these vistas that have become "stifling", a series of winding passages that lead nowhere.[15] The narrator makes it perfectly clear that Dorothea's own blindness is responsible for her self-delusion. Mr. Casaubon, the narrative voice says in a passage contiguous to the one quoted above, "had not actively assisted in creating any illusions about himself".

The fourth and last part of the meditation is a 133 — word sentence. The narrator's syntax has apparently been influenced by the accelerated mental activity he is describing. Nevertheless, this final section of the meditation, in large measure, is objective analysis, at a distance, by the narrator. Dorothea, says the narrative voice in this section, is prevented by her husband's coldness from "pouring forth her girlish and

womanly feeling". The "childlike caresses" she desires to
feast on seem to point to the fact that she has still up to this
point retained her former desire to love and be loved — which,
in fact, she never loses. It is another fixed element of her
nature.

George Eliot makes no explicit comments in these passages
about Dorothea's "education", but it is plain that this
process is being described. Dorothea's mistaken devotion
and blind dutifulness are in large measure also self-gratification,
and she learns this only as she sees into the true natures both
of her husband and herself. Subjectivity, for George Eliot, is
bad because it is in many ways equivalent to self-absorption.
Objectivity, which one acquires only as he perfects the art of
vision — that is, the ability to see clearly beyond one's
self — objectivity is what George Eliot's protagonists must
acquire before they have completed their moral education. In
the passage just examined, Dorothea begins to doubt her
husband for the first time, and in doing so she also begins to
doubt her own judgment for the first time. Her self-doubt
will lead to self-knowledge, and then to a more perceptive
view of her surroundings and her proper role in them.

The relationship between the narrator and the protagonist
in this meditation fluctuates somewhat, as it did in Jane
Austen's novels. George Eliot's narrator, however, is less
self-effacing, more easily located. Her narrator seems, a good
deal of the time, more intrusively present than Jane Austen's
ever is. George Eliot's narrator is extremely sensitive to the
qualities of the protagonist's mind — but he often stands
farther away from the protagonist than Jane Austen's
narrator ever does. That is, George Eliot's narrator is capable
of following the minutest processes of the protagonist's
mind with total sympathy, but he is also capable of detaching
himself from that mind sufficiently to call attention to its
relation to her general character, to other people, and to
mankind in general. Jane Austen's narrative voice never does
these things. George Eliot's is capable of doing any or all of
them at any moment in the novel, and the result is that
Dorothea's mind seems to be expressed in a context that is
wider than Elizabeth Bennet's or Emma Woodhouse's.

The narrator's knowledge, always superior to that of the

protagonist, once again creates a certain irony of presentation. It is ironic that Dorothea cannot see what we, with the help of the narrator, see. But George Eliot's narrative voice, in failing to "withdraw" as often as Jane Austen's, rarely brings about that additional level of irony I have identified as being present in *Emma*. This, I think, is because George Eliot is less interested than Jane Austen in recreating in her narrative structure the confusion of her protagonist's mind than she is interested in drawing from that confusion a wide-ranging statement on the pitfalls of blinding self-absorption. Jane Austen, of course, comments on this subject too, but she seems less concerned to draw any universal lessons out of it than to define its importance for her own particular characters. She implies that her lessons have general significance, but she does not say that they do, as George Eliot's narrative voice so often does. The result, in George Eliot's novels, is a more consistently fluctuating distance between the narrative presence and the characters it describes, a phenomenon that helps generate an almost ubiquitous irony. George Eliot's irony, as I have suggested, is not so complex a thing as Jane Austen's is, but it is no less present. Even when George Eliot's narrator follows the psychological processes of the heroine very closely, we as readers, with the help of the narrator, can see beyond them — that is, we can see more than the protagonist herself because of the knowledge we have already acquired through the omniscient mind surrounding the protagonist's mind. Our knowledge, which parallels for the most part that of the narrator, can expand with his into the realm of general overview, and so we often find ourselves, in George Eliot's novels — as in Jane Austen's — knowing more than the characters know. However, as I have suggested, George Eliot's narrator is for the most part a more opaque presence than Jane Austen's, and so the irony, while consistent, is less multi-dimensional. George Eliot's irony is more usually a form of traditional dramatic irony, an irony resulting from the narrator's superior knowledge and judgment in relation to the characters, a superiority he nevertheless sometimes abstains from acknowledging in order to get as close as possible to the mind of the protagonist. Thus George Eliot's irony on the one hand, and the continuously fluctuating distance between the narrator and the characters on the other, are very closely related — are, in fact, virtually interdependent.

Dorothea's second meditation occurs shortly after she and Mr. Casaubon return from their honeymoon and establish themselves at Lowick Manor. By this time Dorothea has become more fully disillusioned with her husband and her marriage, but the fatal depth of her former blindness is not as yet completely clear to her. It becomes clearer in a sudden flash as he returns to her room. Her "education" approaches its climax, and what follows in the novel is more or less the dénouement, the direct result, as it were, of Dorothea's new objectivity.

The duties of her married life, contemplated as so great beforehand, seemed to be shrinking with the furniture and the white-vapour-welled landscape.(1) The clear heights where she expected to walk in full communion had become difficult to see even in her imagination; the delicious repose of the soul on a complete superior had been shaken into uneasy effort and alarmed with dim presentiment.(2) When would the days begin of that active wifely devotion which was to strengthen her husband's life and exalt her own?(3) Never, perhaps, as she had preconceived them; but somehow — still somehow.(4) In this solemnly pledged union of her life, duty would present itself in some new form of inspiration and give a new meaning to wifely love.(5)

Meanwhile there was the snow and the low arch of dun vapour — there was the stifling oppression of that gentlewoman's world, where everything was done for her and none asked for her aid — where the sense of connection with a manifold pregnant existence had to be kept up painfully as an inward vision, instead of coming from without in claims that would have shaped her energies. — 'What shall I do?' 'Whatever you please, my dear': that had been her brief history since she had left off learning morning lessons and practising silly rhythms on the hated piano.(6) Marriage, which was to bring guidance into worthy and imperative occupation, had not yet freed her from the gentlewoman's oppressive liberty; it had not even filled her leisure with the ruminant joy of unchecked tenderness.(7) Her blooming full-pulsed youth stood there in a moral imprisonment which made itself one with the chill, colourless, narrowed landscape, with the shrunken furniture, the never-read books, and the ghostly stag in a pale fantastic world that seemed to be vanishing from the daylight.(8)

In the first minutes when Dorothea looked out she felt nothing but the dreary oppression; then came a keen remembrance, and turning away from the window she walked round the room.(9) The ideas and hopes which were living in her mind when she first saw this room nearly three months before were present now only as memories; she judged

them as we judge transient and departed things.(10) All existence
seemed to beat with a lower pulse than her own, and her religious faith
was a solitary cry, the struggle out of a nightmare in which every object
was withering and shrinking away from her.(11) Each remembered
thing in the room was disenchanted, was deadened as an unlit
transparency, till her wandering gaze came to the group of miniatures,
and there at last she saw something which had gathered new breath
and meaning: it was the miniature of Mr. Casaubon's aunt Julia, who had
made the unfortunate marriage — of Will Ladislaw's grandmother.(12)
Dorothea could fancy that it was alive now — the delicate woman's face
which had yet a headstrong look, a peculiarity difficult to interpret.(13)
Was it only her friends who thought her marriage unfortunate? or did
she herself find it out to be a mistake, and taste the salt bitterness of her
tears in the merciful silence of the night?(14) What breadths of
experience Dorothea seemed to have passed over since she first looked
at this miniature!(15) She felt a new companionship with it, as if it had
an ear for her and could see how she was looking at it.(16)Here was a
woman who had known some difficulty about marriage.(17) Nay, the
colours deepened, the lips and chin seemed to get larger, the hair and
eyes seemed to be sending out light, the face was masculine and
beamed on her with that full gaze which tells her on whom it falls that
she is too interesting for the slightest movement of her eyelid to pass
unnoticed and uninterpreted.(18) The vivid presentation came like a
pleasant glow to Dorothea; she felt herself smiling, and turning from
the miniature sat down and looked up as if she were again talking to a
figure in front of her.(19) But the smile disappeared as she went on
meditating . . . .(20)[16]

Dorothea meditates as she scans the world from the
window of her room.[17] What is suggested throughout this
passage is her imprisonment, the contraction of her hopes
and expectations, the shrinkage of her vistas. The word
"oppression", for example, is used three times. At the end
of her meditation, as she begins to recognize the nature of
her former blindness, Dorothea has a "vivid presentation", a
sudden but as yet not totally complete realization of the
presumably reciprocal feelings that exist between herself and
Will Ladislaw and thus by implication of the true nature of
her relationship with her husband and of her own lack of
judgment in marrying him. Her realization comes partly as
a result of her vision of Will at the end of the meditation,
but she does not fully understand the situation at this point.
Her former blind faith in duty, which is also a form of self-
gratification, is now insufficient of itself to sustain her.

The image of "shrinking" occurs in the very first sentence
of the meditation. Her physical surroundings seem to

Dorothea to have contracted, a contraction that suggests that
things at Lowick look smaller to her after her travels and
implies further that the state of her mind in regard to her
husband and her marriage continues to undergo substantial
alteration. The seeming contraction of her physical
surroundings makes Dorothea feel trapped. Once again a
mental condition is expressed in terms of a topographical
setting, and once again the relationship between the character
and her environment is expressed principally in epistemological terms. Dorothea discovers, upon her return to Lowick,
that she has nothing to do. Her religious needs, her reforming
zeal, her desire to love and be loved — all of these things
must remain unsatisfied in a world that cannot satisfy them
and in marriage to a man who cannot sympathize with them.
While the reader may understand these images of shrinking
and contraction metaphorically, for Dorothea the shrinking
and contraction are literal, literally true. Her experience of
not having anything to do becomes a parallel or concomitant
of the experience of detachment from the physical world. A
world in which social engagement and meaningful involvement
are impossible also becomes a world, in other words, in which
one experiences the physical as being something literally dark
and stifling. It is Dorothea's married experience that
determines her epistemological relationship to Lowick and its
environs in this passage. The same motif is continued in the
second sentence of the meditation, in which Dorothea's
original idea of what her marriage would be like is expressed
in the phrase "the clear heights where she expected to walk in
full communion". But now, continuing the image, these
heights have become "difficult to see", and all that is left to
Dorothea is a "dim presentiment" of disaster. One of the
striking things about the figures of speech here is their
constant emphasis on the subject of *vision*. Such words as
"contemplated", "clear", "see", and "dim" keep reminding
the reader that the problem Dorothea has to overcome is that
of faulty vision; learning to "see" is the most important step
down the road of her education. And yet, in sentence five,
she is still suffering from her martyr complex enough to be
pursuing some illusory, metaphysical form of "duty".
Ironically, the "new meaning to wifely love" will become

manifest to her in an unexpected way shortly.

The sixth sentence continues the comparison between exterior topography and Dorothea's mental condition; the "snow and the low arch of dun vapour" become the objective expression or embodiment for Dorothea of "the stifling oppression" of her "gentlewoman's world", in which there is nothing to do. The phrase "stifling oppression" continues the image of shrinking and contraction — of imprisonment, in short — in regard to Dorothea's view of her marriage and the impossibility of satisfying her religious needs when she has nothing to do.

In the seventh sentence the narrative voice reiterates this same idea in mentioning the "oppressive liberty" Dorothea has not been able to get "free" of. The eighth sentence returns once again to the idea of contraction, of shrinking, of eclipse. Dorothea's condition is labelled here that of "moral imprisonment", an imprisonment that is explicitly linked, through her experience of her physical surroundings, with what she sees beyond the window — that is, "the chill, colourless, narrowed landscape". The moral landscape has narrowed along with the physical one, and each is expressed in terms of the other once again. The basis of this linkage, as I have suggested, is the feeling of psychological contraction and darkness with which Dorothea views her environment. However, as the "pale fantastic world" seems to be "vanishing from the daylight", Dorothea's "vision" seems to have begun to penetrate the depths of her mistake. The light-dark dichotomy is again applied to the educative process, and the way is now prepared for the "vivid presentation" to Dorothea of her own folly.

Sentences nine and ten relate Dorothea's recollection of the last time she saw the room she now occupies and the discrepancy between her expectations then and the present reality that is now manifest to her. The phrase "dreary oppression" keeps the leitmotif before the reader. The eleventh sentence continues the idea of the "shrinking" and "withering" of Dorothea's "vistas".[18] The phrase "struggle out of a nightmare" repeats the image of sentence eight; Dorothea's world seems to her "to be vanishing from the daylight." The same image reappears in the next sentence,

sentence twelve; the objects in the room are "deadened to an unlit transparency". The image of fading light is the dominant one in this section of the novel, and George Eliot uses it as an emblem for Dorothea's "disenchantment". Her lack of engagement in the world, a vocation, something to do, someone to love, makes the physical world seem to shrink away from her, to shroud itself in darkness. The darkness, which is a literal darkness for Dorothea, becomes for the reader a metaphor both for disillusionment and for moral blindness; Dorothea must err before she attains objectivity, just as the darkness precedes the day.

In this part of the meditation Dorothea is brooding specifically on the subject of her "unfortunate marriage", and so the picture of Mr. Casaubon's Aunt Julia — Will Ladislaw's grandmother, who also made an "unfortunate marriage" — acts on her mind both as a suggestion and as a reinforcement. The connection between Aunt Julia's marriage and Dorothea's own is emphasized by the narrative voice in sentence thirteen. Dorothea fancies the face "alive now"; the face looks "headstrong", which is an adjective of course as easily applied to Dorothea herself, whose marriage to Mr. Casaubon took place in defiance of good advice from friends and relatives and was largely the result of her own stubbornness.[19] Such stubbornness is "a peculiarity difficult to interpret" because it is also Dorothea's peculiarity, and few of us are good at self-analysis.

Sentences fifteen and sixteen indicate that the screw has been turned; Dorothea's feeling of "new companionship" with the face in the miniature tells the reader that she now admits to herself that she has made an unfortunate marriage. It is the first time in the novel that Dorothea is so candid, and yet the revelation is not expressed in direct terms. The narrator does not say that Dorothea is now sorry she married Mr. Casaubon; instead it is shown to the reader that Dorothea's discovery is gradual and fragmentary, and that it is in the image of another person similar to herself that she sees her own reflection. Dorothea now "looks" at the picture differently; it is of course the same picture, but she herself has changed. As was the case in the meditations in Jane Austen's novels, nothing physical has actually happened here — the heroine merely thinks, and in thinking learns.

Dorothea continues to gaze at the miniature of Aunt Julia. Here are two women who have "known some difficulty about marriage". In the eighteenth sentence the narrative voice takes up once again the dark-light metaphor and even puns on the subject. Aunt Julia's face, which seems to Dorothea to become momentarily the face of Will Ladislaw, is described here as "sending out light" and "beaming" upon Dorothea. The face in the miniature shines upon Dorothea, and it is also a major means by which Dorothea literally sees the light. Aunt Julia's mistake reminds her of her own, which was to marry Mr. Casaubon instead of his nephew. Out of the darkness of error comes the light of knowledge. There is no danger that such light will "pass unnoticed and uninterpreted". It is being interpreted at the present time. Thus, in the nineteenth sentence, "The vivid presentation came like a pleasant glow to Dorothea". She smiles at her vivid presentation and at the thought of herself once again in conversation with Will; yet, at the end, the smile disappears "as she went on meditating", in the following passages to discover, with even more vivid clarity of insight, how really disastrous a mistake she has made and how far her egoism has led her astray. Her self-comprehension is not as yet total; the narrator seems to know that Dorothea is in love with Will, but she herself does not as yet understand this completely. Nevertheless, a realization of past error does seem at this point very much present to her.

George Eliot's protagonists, unlike Jane Austen's, often think in terms of analogies. Dorothea sees things in terms of other things; she even sees herself in terms of someone else. This helps explain why George Eliot's language is often metaphorical in passages dealing in such analytical detail with a character's thoughts.[20] As she says in *The Mill on the Floss* (Book II, Chapter 1), "We can . . . seldom declare what a thing is, except by saying it is something else". This, perhaps, helps explain George Eliot's penchant for viewing her characters not only as individuals but also as universal types — that is, as illustrations of various universal truths about human nature as she conceives it. This is why her narrator frequently calls attention to the relationship of Dorothea's mind to her general character, to the minds of other people, and to mankind in general. This aspect of George Eliot's narrative technique is one way in which she is different from Jane Austen, as I have suggested. And yet Dorothea's educative process is similar in many ways to those of Elizabeth Bennet and Emma Woodhouse, and receives its impetus from similar stimuli.

Even more consistently than in Jane Austen's novels, George Eliot's narrator seems to stay in control of the language. Dorothea's mind, more often than Elizabeth's or Emma's, is tactfully represented by the mind copresent with it, the ubiquitous surrounding mind of the narrator. The narrator's presence in *Middlemarch* is more obtrusive, in other words, than is the narrator's presence in *Pride and Prejudice* or *Emma*. This is because George Eliot's narrator, as I have said, is more prone than Jane Austen's to detach himself from the protagonist and to comment upon the general and even the universal applications the workings and nature of the protagonist's mind have in a world in which both human nature and the hard facts of existence are fixed, and changeable only with great effort.

Finally, it seems apparent that Dorothea is just as logical and articulate in her mental crisis as Jane Austen's heroines are in theirs. A major difference between her and them, however, is that Dorothea has less insight. She reasons logically, but from the wrong premises — premises assuming, for example, that her religious needs can be fulfilled in the world she lives in, and that marriage to Mr. Casaubon will be an avenue to religious fulfillment as well as a satisfactory channeling of her desire to love and be loved. Jane Austen's heroines make mistakes because they are blinded by puzzling data — that is, they have the proper evidence for making the right decisions, but they assemble their evidence erroneously due to self-absorption. Dorothea's "evidence", her "data", is really non-evidence, non-data; her egoism blinds her and causes her both to invent things that are never really there and to ignore things that are.

Once again there is an ironic discrepancy between the protagonist's state of enlightenment and that of the reader, who is enabled to see the true state of affairs through the detachment of the novel's omniscient narrator. The additional level of irony I have identified as being present in Jane Austen's novels, however, is lacking in *Middlemarch* because the narrator's detachment in that novel is more substantial and consistent — which helps give rise, as I have also suggested, to the continuously fluctuating ironic distance between the narrator and the characters with whom he is, from various perspectives, concerned.

III

Daniel Deronda contains some of George Eliot's greatest writing and also some of her worst. This was the assessment made by F.R. Leavis two decades ago, and it is, I think, entirely correct.[21] Recent critical opinion has tended more or less to accept this judgment. Leavis went so far as to say in his essay that the Gwendolen Harleth half of the novel should be published separately and the rest of it scrapped. He later recanted, admitting that the Daniel plot and the Gwendolen plot are in some ways symbiotic, but his early comment is symptomatic of the first response of many readers. The Daniel Deronda part of the novel (mostly the latter half) is excruciatingly dull; it is ponderous, abstract, unreal, and even in places carelessly written. There have of course been some explanations offered for this failure. I think the best one is the simplest: George Eliot's real talent lay in her treatment of the ordinary; in dealing with the extraordinary, in this novel represented by the Jewish or Zionist parts, she had to strain, to read up, to submerge her usual spontaneity of treatment in a plethora of footnotes.

I also agree with Leavis when he says that the Gwendolen half of *Daniel Deronda* (mostly the first half) represents some of George Eliot's best work. Leavis is surely right in his admiration for George Eliot's treatment of Gwendolen; perhaps no other character in English fiction has her thoughts, her ideas, her motives, so minutely anatomized.[22]

I have indicated that there are perhaps reasons for treating the two halves of the novel differently. There is, however, at least one basic similarity between Daniel Deronda and Gwendolen Harleth. Deronda, the disinherited intellectual, goes through roughly the same three stages Gwendolen goes through, those consecutive stages of egoism, despair, and final objectivity which almost all of George Eliot's protagonists experience. Gwendolen's "education", for example, recalls Adam Bede's. Both suffer for their egoism, and both are ultimately the better for their suffering. Gwendolen is another of George Eliot's tragic heroines who are made miserable by their blindness in order that they may at last see. Her tragedy arises out of the conflict within her of pride and sensitivity on the one hand and false values and self-ignorance on the other.

At the center of this novel is the question of what is real and good and what is not. Once again it is the art of *vision* that must be cultivated in order to see the answer to this all-encompassing question. The question of appearance and reality, of blindness and truth, keeps reappearing, for example, in the continuing series of references to the theater. Theater images are often used in connection not only with Gwendolen but also with such supporting characters as Daniel's mother, Mirah, and Klesmer.

In *Daniel Deronda* George Eliot focuses on the aristocracy for a longer time than in any other of her novels, but in other respects the situation of her heroine is somewhat similar to that of Dorothea in *Middlemarch*. Gwendolen, like Dorothea, makes a bad marriage, and her moral direction afterwards is typical in many ways of most of George Eliot's protagonists. Gwendolen's blind egoism becomes, through education, objectivity and self-awareness. She even acquires a modicum of the sympathy for her fellow men with which Dorothea began her struggle and on the subject of which George Eliot was always at her most eloquent and appealing.

Gwendolen indulges in two rather elaborate retrospective meditations, the first of which occurs during Grandcourt's courting of her.[23] She is both repelled and fascinated by him, as by a serpent (an image applied to him frequently) — repelled by the obviously insidious nature of his character, fascinated by his money, his social status, and his courtly manners. Throughout the first half of the novel, and until she finally marries him, Gwendolen periodically debates with herself the question of whether or not she should accept

Grandcourt when he proposes (she is always sure he will). He finally does so by letter, and she resolves to refuse him when he comes to call. He calls, but she is unable to refuse him after all; the comparisons she must make between the struggles of her mother and herself to live comfortably, and his grandeur and ease, weigh heavily upon her, and all her resolutions to refuse him finally recede.

Gwendolen's motives are constantly assessed and reassessed by the surrounding narrative voice. Here is part of her first meditation, which takes place on the day Grandcourt comes to receive from her an answer to his proposal of marriage.

Through the last twenty hours, with a brief interruption of sleep, she had been so occupied with perpetually alternating images and arguments for and against the possibility of her marrying Grandcourt, that the conclusion which she had determined on beforehand ceased to have any hold on her consciousness: the alternate dip of counterbalancing thoughts begotten of counterbalancing desires had brought her into a state in which no conclusion could look fixed to her. She would have expressed her resolve as before; but it was a form out of which the blood had been sucked — no more a part of quivering life than the 'God's will be done' of one who is eagerly watching chances. She did not mean to accept Grandcourt; from the first moment of receiving his letter she had meant to refuse him; still, that could not but prompt her to look the unwelcome reasons full in the face until she had a little less awe of them, could not hinder her imagination from filling out her knowledge in various ways, some of which seemed to change the aspect of what she knew. By dint of looking at a dubious object with a constructive imagination, one can give it twenty different shapes.

* * * * * * *

But now — did she know exactly what was the state of the case with regard to Mrs. Glasher and her children? She had given a sort of promise — had said, 'I will not interfere with your wishes.' But would another woman who married Grandcourt be in fact the decisive obstacle to her wishes, or be doing her and her boy any real injury? Might it not be just as well, nay better, that Grandcourt should marry? For what could not a woman do when she was married, if she knew how to assert herself? Here all was constructive imagination. Gwendolen had about as accurate a conception of marriage — that is to say, of the mutual influences, demands, duties of man and woman in the state of matrimony — as she had of magnetic currents and the law of storms.

* * * * * * *

Gwendolen had found no objection to Grandcourt's way of being enamoured before she had had that glimpse of his past, which she resented as if it had been a deliberate offence against her.(1) His advances to *her* were deliberate, and she felt a retrospective disgust for them.(2) Perhaps other men's lives were of the same kind — full of secrets which made the ignorant suppositions of the woman they wanted to marry a farce at which they were laughing in their sleeves.(3)

These feelings of disgust and indignation had sunk deep; and though other troublous experience in the last weeks had dulled them from passion into remembrance, it was chiefly their reverberating activity which kept her firm to the understanding with herself, that she was not going to accept Grandcourt.(4) She had never meant to form a new determination; she had only been considering what might be thought or said.(5) If anything could have induced her to change, it would have been the prospect of making all things easy for 'poor mamma': that, she admitted, was a temptation.(6) But no! she was going to refuse him.(7) Meanwhile, the thought that he was coming to be refused was inspiriting: she had the white reins in her hands again; there was a new current in her frame, reviving her from the beaten-down consciousness in which she had been left by the interview with Klesmer.(8) She was not now going to crave an opinion of her capabilities; she was going to exercise her power.(9)

Was this what made her heart palpitate annoyingly when she heard the horse's footsteps on the gravel? — when Miss Merry, who opened the door to Grandcourt, came to tell her that he was in the drawing-room? (10) The hours of preparation and the triumph of the situation were apparently of no use: she might as well have seen Grandcourt coming suddenly on her in the midst of her despondency.(11)[24]

The first section of this meditation redefines for the reader the condition of Gwendolen's mind. She wants to refuse Grandcourt, so she thinks, but she finds it extremely difficult to decide unalterably to do so. The opening sentence of the meditation makes this clear. Gwendolen's "inward debating" with herself, to use a phrase of the narrator's, takes the form of "perpetually alternating images and arguments for and against the possibility of her marrying Grandcourt", a situation which is in turn described by the narrative voice as "the alternate dip of counterbalancing thoughts begotten of counterbalancing desires". Gwendolen's "consciousness" has "brought her into a state in which no conclusion could look fixed". The language of balanced indecision in this sentence ("perpetually alternating", "for and against", "alternate dip", "counterbalancing thoughts", "counterbalancing desires") helps express the vector pull of opposing energies in Gwendolen's mind on the subject of Grandcourt's proposal.[25] This series of contradictory vectors of energy in her mind typifies in many ways the nature of human thought as George Eliot seems to view it in this novel. One way in which the narrative language of her novels differs from that of Jane Austen's is in the prevalence of dynamic or mechanical metaphors for the way the human mind works. Gwendolen constantly balances things in her mind; she is pulled toward marriage and away from it, toward Grandcourt and away from him, toward money and pleasure and ease and away from them. She alternates between sexual desire and repulsion in her thoughts about Grandcourt, as the rest of the meditation makes clear; and, as the narrative voice also makes clear, she vacillates between knowledge (of what Grandcourt is really like) and imagination (how she could change him). George Eliot's picture of the human mind throughout this meditation is a deterministic one of physical forces in conflict, some of which are stronger than others. The balance of these forces may change later on, but Gwendolen, like Dorothea at a similar stage of development, presents to the reader here the image of a nature fixed and capable of yielding to change only with the greatest personal exertion. Her attraction to Grandcourt will ultimately vanquish her repulsion, for example, just as her imagination will triumph over her knowledge. In the same way, after her marriage, Grandcourt will in turn dominate her.

This first section of the meditation further emphasizes these ideas in various ways. "She would have expressed her resolve", but she is not really "resolved" enough to do so. The third sentence is in effect a cornucopia of vacillation. "She did not *mean*" to accept Grandcourt; she always "*meant* to refuse him"; "still", "but", and so forth. Gwendolen's failure to "see", to be objective, is implied here; she seems to be attempting throughout to rationalize an acceptance of Grandcourt's proposal. There is a distinction made here between "imagination" and "knowledge", and it becomes clear that Gwendolen's imagination is capable of "changing the aspect of what she knew. By dint of looking at a dubious object with a constructive imagination", the narrative voice concludes, "one can give it twenty different shapes". Here, then, is George Eliot's epistemology of the imagination and her explanation of the way it works. The imagination is generated primarily by egoism — by personal and selfish desires — and thus it imposes outward a shadow on the world that invents things that are not really there and hides things that are. Dorothea's imagination does the same things. As if to remind the reader of Gwendolen's obfuscation of the real issues, the phrase "constructive imagination" is used again later in the meditation, further emphasizing the ironic distance between the narrator and the protagonist. George Eliot's narrator, as I have suggested, is capable both of a close and sympathetic following of the mind's movements and of speaking from a distant, more generalized perspective. Here, in labelling Gwendolen's obfuscation the result of a constructive imagination, the narrator has backed away in order to be more objective, and thus Gwendolen's thoughts are reported from a perspective ironic both because of its distance and because of the obvious superiority of its clarity and objectivity over her own.

In this section, then, the reader sees Gwendolen's mental struggle expressed in terms of the conflict of opposing forces. He also sees that she is failing to be honest with herself, that she is clouding the real issues at stake by burying the questionable aspects of Grandcourt's character in the rhapsodies of a "constructive imagination". Most of these conclusions are readily obtainable because of the explicitness of the omniscient narrative voice. In this section it not only relates Gwendolen's thoughts in past-tense, third-person description, but, typical of George Eliot's narrative voice, it also detaches itself even further in the last sentence in order to draw a universal moral.

The second section of the meditation defines for the reader precisely what it is that Gwendolen fails to see, defines the mistake in judgment she is going to make and then become aware of only after her marriage, when it is too late for such new insight, too late to admit error. The mistake is essentially Gwendolen's belief that if she were to marry Grandcourt she could neutralize his powerful influence, his tenacious will, by "asserting herself" over him. It is her complete failure to do this later on that precipitates her conjugal misery and that in turn teaches her to know both Grandcourt and herself better. Gwendolen's faith in herself, like Dorothea's private image of herself, is based on a misunderstanding of the facts. Gwendolen's second meditation will make this even clearer.

The second section of this meditation consists mostly of a series of questions Gwendolen asks herself. She attempts through them to rationalize out of existence her promise to Mrs. Glasher not to marry Grandcourt, and her blind egoism reaches a climax when she says to herself, "Might it not be just as well, nay better, that Grandcourt should marry? For what could not a woman do when she was married, if she knew how to assert herself?" At this point, however, the narrative voice somewhat tersely deflates Gwendolen's reasoning: "Here all was constructive imagination". Gwendolen, the narrative voice says, knows nothing whatsoever about "the mutual influences, demands, duties" of men and women who are married, and so of course her self-centered judgment will lead her astray. The narrator presumably knows that whenever Gwendolen's will and Grandcourt's should collide his will will triumph because it is the stronger of the two. This points once again to George Eliot's determinism, the scientism of her approach to human psychology, in which she is essentially different f m Jane Austen. Later on in the novel, when Gwendolen learns that she is unable to "assert herself" over Grandcourt, she finally sees what the reader, with the help of the narrative voice, has seen all along, even before the marriage: that she has been deluding herself. As in Jane Austen's novels and in *Middlemarch*, there is an irony here in the failure of the heroine's understanding to keep pace with that of the narrator and, through him, with that of the reader as well. However, as I have said, there are fewer moments in George Eliot's fiction than in Jane Austen's when the thinking voice of the protagonist actually becomes indistinguishable from that of the narrator, and thus the additional level of irony I have identified as being a radical element of Jane Austen's novels is usually missing in George Eliot's, in *Daniel Deronda* as well as in *Middlemarch*. George Eliot's narrator tends more to distance himself from the fictive personality, for reasons I have already enumerated.

The last sentence of the second section of the meditation contains an interesting analogy. Gwendolen's conception of marriage is said to be about as accurate as her knowledge of "magnetic currents and the law of storms", which suggests that the dynamics of marriage and the relative powers of will of the husband and wife are like natural forces. Gwendolen's will is not as strong as she thinks it is when she plans to "assert herself" over Grandcourt after they are married; Grandcourt's will, instead, turns out to be more powerful. This conception of the conflict of wills further exemplifies the dynamic, mechanical process of interpersonal relations among human beings as George Eliot views it. When two forces collide, the stronger will inevitably dominate the weaker. And so it is with people; one dominates or is domineered over depending upon the relative strength of his will, which is usually a fixed element of his being. The language here is in keeping with the mechanical language of balances in the first section of this meditation and once again further emphasizes the ironic distancing between the narrative presence and the protagonist. George Eliot's narrator, sometimes close to the characters and sometimes far away from them, here takes another step backwards in order to make a generalization the heroine herself is incapable of making because of the inferiority of her understanding. It is another case of dramatic irony generated by the narrative structure.

Gwendolen finds aspects of Grandcourt repugnant, but she wants to marry him anyway in order to escape the boredom and the relative poverty of her life at home with her mother. In the meantime, however, Gwendolen is embarking on her education — and a painful one it will be. Once again the familiar pattern will appear. After her marriage Gwendolen will see how she has misjudged Grandcourt and thus herself and her own capabilities as well — a new sort of vision that will lead to more objectivity in her perspective upon the world she lives in.

In the last sentence of this section the narrative voice detaches itself somewhat from the mind it has been describing and makes a general pronouncement on the nature of Gwendolen's mental processes. Like the narrator of *Middlemarch*, the narrator of *Daniel Deronda,* as I have said, is capable of standing both close and far away from the protagonist, of following her mental activity with close sympathy and also relating it on occasion to her general character, to other people, and to the rest of the world.

In the third and final part of this meditation the reader sees the result of the warring vectors of energy within Gwendolen's mind. When Grandcourt actually comes, the war ends. His attraction for her wins out. Gwendolen will marry Grandcourt, knowing what she does about him, to indulge her desire for comfort and status, and also, of course, to indulge the attraction she feels for him. She thinks she can neutralize his powerful will after they are married. Of course, as it ironically turns out, Grandcourt consistently makes her uncomfortable, reduces her to the state of a dependent, and generally illuminates for her the weakness of her will and her own lack of foresight in this regard.

In the first sentence of the third section Gwendolen's feelings about Grandcourt's alliance with Mrs. Glasher, and his brutal termination of it, are defined. George Eliot uses the phrase "retrospective disgust" to describe Gwendolen's attitude in sentence two; almost everything that Gwendolen thinks about in this meditation she thinks about retrospectively. She thinks, in other words, in the same way as Elizabeth Bennet, Emma Woodhouse, and Dorothea Brooke in this respect — in terms of the past and its possible effects on the present and the future. In the third sentence she comes closest to approaching truth. Here Gwendolen visualizes, momentarily, Grandcourt's real nature. He is certainly enamored of her, but he wants more than anything else to conquer and possess her in order to satiate his pride and passion for ownership.[26] Gwendolen does not realize all of this, but she does wonder how many "ignorant suppositions" she may have about Grandcourt's real motives. Later on, of course, her knowledge of his character will be more sadly complete.

Gwendolen's feelings of repugnance, in the fourth sentence, have "sunk deep", and though they have recently been "dulled . . . from passion into remembrance", they keep "reverberating" through her mind. It is this "reverberating" quality of thought that George Eliot seems so intent on reproducing; she attempts to picture for the reader Gwendolen's constant "counterbalancing" of arguments leading one way with arguments leading the other — that is, her "inward debating", the constant conflict of the physical forces of her mind. The reverberation of these "feelings of disgust and indignation", further, is what keeps Gwendolen "firm to the understanding with herself" that she is going to refuse Grandcourt, so the reader is told. Yet this phrase, as soon as it is delivered, is immediately undercut by the equivocation of the very next sentence, which epitomizes neatly the "reverberation" of these "counterbalancing" ideas in Gwendolen's mind. For the fifth sentence reads: "She had never meant to form a new determination; she had only been considering what might be thought or said". The obvious lack of resolution in this sentence is further substantiated by the next one, which begins: "If anything could have induced her to change . . . ." Then comes, once again, the usual rationalization: if she married Grandcourt she could make things easy for 'poor mamma' ". This is a rather euphemistic way of saying that she could make things easy for herself, at least financially, and this is why, at the end of the sixth sentence, such a decision is labelled in advance a "temptation" that Gwendolen is in the act of "admitting". Then, in the seventh sentence, the pendulum swings back the other way: "But no! she was going to refuse him". Despite that exclamation the reader senses that while Gwendolen says she is going to refuse Grandcourt, what she is really saying is that once again she "means" to refuse him, or wishes she could refuse him. These constantly warring desires, expressed in images of vacillation and indecision, further emphasize George Eliot's dynamic conception of human psychology.

At the end of the meditation, Gwendolen once more assures herself that she can withstand Grandcourt's assault, and she almost welcomes another opportunity to assert herself over him, or to try to. Her resolves, however, collapse like a pyramid of cards when Grandcourt actually arrives, as the final two sentences indicate. The picture of Gwendolen one sees at the end of the meditation is that of despondent defeat. She is unable to resist Grandcourt, mostly because she does not really want to resist him. She will give in, and she knows it. The "alternate dip of counterbalancing desires" has ended; that psychic vector of energy representing

Gwendolen's attraction to Grandcourt and to what he embodies has won out, and the pendulum rests on marriage after all. This result also foreshadows what will happen after her marriage; Gwendolen will continue to cave in whenever there is any conflict of desires or wills.

Gwendolen's decision is a result of her own weakness. She suspects that Grandcourt will not be an ideal husband, but she believes that she can control him when necessary, and she wants to be rescued from her present social and pecuniary embarrassments. Gwendolen's inner conflict is what George Eliot defines in *The Mill on the Floss* (Book 4, Chapter 2) as that "between the inward impulse and outward fact, which is the lot of every imaginative and passionate nature . . . ." And so she marries him. As one can see from this meditation, it is an act of egoism and blindness — egoistic in the sense that it is above all self-gratifying (although Gwendolen also genuinely wants to relieve her mother from financial worry), blind in the sense that Gwendolen is a far weaker person than Grandcourt and ought to see that this is the case. But, like Dorothea, Gwendolen has been blinded to her own nature by her self-absorption and must be educated in the art of vision before she can begin to see more objectively. And like Daniel Deronda, whose story occupies the other half of this novel, Gwendolen must suffer before she is "saved".

When the reader encounters Gwendolen again it is after her marriage; her apprenticeship in suffering, her education, has begun in earnest. She has become aware of her husband's terrible strength and of her own folly. Like Dorothea, she feels trapped. Once again the heroine begins to discover herself after she has become aware of misjudging a male protagonist.

Poor Gwendolen was conscious of an uneasy, transforming process — all the old nature shaken to its depths, its hopes spoiled, its pleasures perturbed, but still showing wholeness and strength in the will to reassert itself.(1) After every new shock of humiliation she tried to adjust herself and seize her old supports — proud concealment, trust in new excitement that would make life go by without much thinking; trust in some deed of reparation to nullify her self-blame and shield her from a vague, ever-visiting dread of some horrible calamity; trust in the hardening effect of use and wont that would make her indifferent to her miseries.(2)

Yes — miseries.(3) This beautiful, healthy young creature, with her two-and-twenty years and her gratified ambition, no longer felt inclined to kiss her fortunate image in the glass; she looked at it with wonder that she could be so miserable.(4) One belief which had accompanied her through her unmarried life as a self-cajoling superstition, encouraged by the subordination of everyone about her — the belief in her own power of dominating — was utterly gone.(5) Already, in seven short weeks, which seemed half her life, her husband had gained a mastery which she could no more resist than she could have resisted the benumbing effect from the touch of a torpedo.(6) Gwendolen's will had seemed imperious in its small girlish way; but it was the will of a creature with a large discourse of imaginative fears: a shadow would have been enough to relax its hold.(7) And she had found a will like that of a crab or a boa-constrictor which goes on pinching or crushing without alarm at thunder.(8) Not that Grandcourt was without calculation of the intangible effects which were the chief means of mastery; indeed he had a surprising acuteness in detecting that situation of feeling in Gwendolen which made her proud and rebellious spirit dumb and helpless before him.(9)

*   *   *   *   *   *   *

And endurance seemed easier than the mortal humiliation of confessing that she knew all before she married him, and in marrying him had broken her word. For the reasons by which she had justified herself when the marriage tempted her, and all her easy arrangement of her future power over her husband to make him do better than he might be inclined to do, were now as futile as the burnt-out lights which set off a child's pageant. Her sense of being blameworthy was exaggerated by a dread both definite and vague. The definite dread was lest the veil of secrecy should fall between her and Grandcourt and give him the right to taunt her. With the reading of [Lydia Glasher's] letter had begun her husband's empire of fear.

*   *   *   *   *   *   *

Gwendolen, indeed, with all that gnawing trouble in her consciousness, had hardly for a moment dropped the sense that it was her part to bear herself with dignity, and appear what is called happy.(1) In disclosure of disappointment or sorrow she saw nothing but a humiliation which would have been vinegar to her wounds.(2) Whatever her husband might come at last to be to her, she meant to wear the yoke so as not to be pitied.(3) For she did think of the coming years with presentiment: she was frightened at Grandcourt.(4) The poor thing had passed from her girlish sauciness of superiority over this inert specimen of personal distinction into an amazed perception of her former ignorance about the possible mental attitude of a man towards the woman he sought in marriage — of her present ignorance as to what their life with each other might turn into.(5) For novelty gives immeasurableness to fear, and fills the early time of all sad changes with phantoms of the future.(6) Her little coquetries, voluntary or involuntary, had told on Grandcourt during courtship, and formed a medium of communication between them, showing him in the light of a creature

such as she could understand and manage: but marriage had nullified all
such interchange, and Grandcourt had become a blank uncertainty to
her in everything but this, that he would do just what he willed, and
that she had neither devices at her command to determine his will, nor
any rational means of escaping it.(7)[27]

Gwendolen has suffered the disappointments of an extensive
education since the reader last saw her. Nevertheless, as the
first sentence of the first section shows, she has not yet
completely given herself up to despair. Her "old nature",
though "shaken to its depths", still retains, so she thinks,
some of its original and indigenous assertiveness. Still, the
image of closing vistas begins to reappear here in the
"spoiled hopes" and "perturbed pleasures" mentioned by the
narrative voice. The last word of the second sentence describes
Gwendolen's current state of mind, and that same word
("Miseries") is picked up again at the beginning of the next
paragraph. What the sentence tells the reader is that
Gwendolen is still gamely trying to resist the sense of
calamity she is laboring under as a result of her marriage to
Grandcourt; she has reached a point, in other words, similar
to Dorothea's during her first meditation in Rome. The phrase
"self-blame" indicates that Gwendolen is beginning to see
more clearly her past folly, the folly of imagining that her
will was strong enough to resist Grandcourt's. The plunge in
"misery", of course, constitutes the second stage in George
Eliot's three-stage process of education (egoism-despair-
vision), and this is where the reader finds Gwendolen during
the present scene. Her education, like Dorothea's, is a painful
one indeed. Sentence four repeats the assertion of
Gwendolen's "misery", and contains a certain gloating tone
characteristic of George Eliot's narrative voice when dealing
with beautiful women. Gwendolen's beauty (like Hetty
Sorrel's in *Adam Bede)* is a cause of her ultimate unhappiness,
and the narrative voice unreservedly points this out. Gwendolen has "gratified" her social "ambitions", but she is still
miserable. Why? Because, as the next sentence and the rest
of the passage make clear, she has misjudged both herself and
her husband, misjudged their relative strengths. It is this error
in judgment that leads to the beginning of her education in
earnest. Gwendolen's "belief in her own power of dominating"

is in the process of disappearing. Before her marriage she felt that she could, if necessary, assert her will over Grandcourt's and so protect herself from her future husband's encroachments upon her freedom. Misjudging both herself and Grandcourt, she finds the situation exactly reversed. Grandcourt has mastered her, and she has become almost will-less.

If "Gwendolen's will had seemed imperious", as the seventh sentence says, it had seemed so primarily to herself. In the blindness of her egoism, she did not dream how easily her will could be destroyed by a man determined to destroy it. Now, however, she has begun to see the truth: she cannot resist Grandcourt's will. This is another example of the determined, fixed aspect of things in George Eliot's world. The phrase "girlish way" continues the idea that Gwendolen's former opinion of her powers was formulated in ignorance. Like Dorothea, she has reasoned from a false premise (the assertiveness of her will) and has landed in the midst of a disaster brought about primarily through the inventiveness and inaccuracy of her imagination. If "a shadow would have been enough" to dissipate her assertiveness, Grandcourt certainly has no trouble dissipating it. The "shadow" once more brings to the reader's attention the play on light and darkness; Grandcourt, of course, is more than a mere shadow — the imagery makes it clear, later on, that he is to be associated with the Prince of Darkness himself.

The imagery of the eighth sentence is interesting and crucial. Grandcourt is pictured to the heroine's mind's eye as a serpent in a garden; for Gwendolen his will is like "that of a crab or a boa-constrictor which goes on pinching or crushing" indefinitely. The imagery applied to Grandcourt here, like that applied to Mr. Casaubon, is that of contraction, shrinking, strangulation, and darkness.[28] Grandcourt, as the last sentence of this section tells the reader, seems particularly adept at anticipating Gwendolen's wishes and frustrating them either directly or obliquely. Her "proud and rebellious spirit", so much her mainstay and her hope before her marriage, is powerless to defeat or even to confront Grandcourt.

The central dynamic structure of this section of the

meditation presents human beings in terms of mechanical or at least physical energies — one energy of will against another stronger energy of will and therefore incapable of asserting itself without great effort. Gwendolen can no more resist Grandcourt's will than she can resist the "benumbing" effects of touching a "torpedo" (electric eel), another image which emphasizes both Gwendolen's helplessness and Grand-court's serpentine power. The narrative voice, from the distance of its ironic perspective on the action of the novel, unreservedly makes these points for the benefit of the reader, who, with the help of the narrator, has seen Grandcourt more clearly than Gwendolen does for some time, and knows long before she does that her will cannot surmount his. Gwendolen, ironically enough, is finally beginning to learn what the reader and the narrator have known all along — that her will is powerless to protect her against Grandcourt's, because his will is stronger. This physical, deterministic view is perhaps a concomitant of the Victorian idea of the husband as master — both domestically and sexually. The female is the victim in both contexts, a casualty of the battle of wills.

This section further supports the idea of the mind as a series of mechanical structures by suggesting that as time goes by the various physical elements in balance within a single soul may change. George Eliot's characters may have fixed natures, but their natures are capable of some alteration. The first five sentences intimate that one of the effects marriage has had upon Gwendolen is that of weakening her self-assurance. She no longer feels confident either in her will or in her luck; she now reacts rather than acts.

Gwendolen had already compromised herself before her marriage, as the opening sentence of the second section of this meditation reminds the reader. Mrs. Glasher had described to her in precise and accurate terms Grandcourt's real character, and Gwendolen in turn had promised, for the sake of Mrs. Glasher's son (fathered by Grandcourt), not to marry him. Grandcourt's knowledge of all of this has given him another distinct advantage over her, for he can make it appear to her without saying so that he knows her motives for marrying him were in some part mercenary and that therefore it is only right that he should regard her as merely another of his possessions.

The serpent imagery in relation to Grandcourt introduced in the preceding section of the meditation is recalled in the second sentence of this one by the phrase "the marriage tempted her". The verb is not capricious; rather it is in keeping with the Satanic imagery applied to Grandcourt throughout.[29] The characterization of Gwendolen's expectations as now "burnt-out lights which set off a child's pageant" is crucial. Grandcourt, like Casaubon, is often portrayed as the human equivalent of darkness, and the metaphorical play of light and darkness in Dorothea's meditations is central to an understanding of his meaning to her.[30] The phrase has further connections with *Middlemarch* (as well as with passages in *Daniel Deronda* already examined). For example, in Dorothea's first meditation the reader is told that one of the things she needs most and misses so much is the opportunity to "feed her affection with those childlike caresses which are the bent of every sweet woman". Gwendolen, though she differs from Dorothea in some ways, desires as Dorothea does to love and be loved. In both cases marriage has made these desires impossible of fulfillment. Thus the lights go out for Gwendolen just as they do for Dorothea; her existence seems to her bleak and unpromising, and this inevitably affects the way she views the physical world. In Dorothea's second meditation it is said of her:

Her blooming full-pulsed youth stood there in a moral imprisonment which made itself one with the chill, colourless, narrowed landscape, with the shrunken furniture, the never-read books, and the ghostly stag in a pale fantastic world that seemed to be vanishing from the daylight . . . . Each remembered thing in the room was disenchanted, was deadened as an unlit transparency . . . .

Both Dorothea and Gwendolen find their environments psychologically darker as a result of their disastrous marriages and shrunken expectations.

The last few sentences of this second section define more clearly Gwendolen's fear of Grandcourt's knowledge of her acquaintance with Mrs. Glasher and all that such an acquaintance would imply. She is beginning to acquire a "sense of being blameworthy" now, and part of her discomfort is a result of "dread both definite and vague". That is to say, the temporal structure of this section involves the future as well as the past. Gwendolen's knowledge of what has already happened to her infects her with a further dread of the future, and presumably it is the "vague" aspect of her dread that is most horrifying. What more will happen to her? The more she worries the more helpless and miserable she feels, and thus her former confidence in the assertive power of her will continues to evaporate. The balance of the elements of her mind, as I have suggested, is capable of alteration with the passage of time. Grandcourt, like Casaubon, has established an "empire of fear" which both constricts his wife and teaches her to see herself and the rest of the world with more objectivity.

The third and final section of this meditation clarifies for the reader a good many of the things I have been describing as radical to the meditation scenes in these novels. Like Elizabeth Bennet, Emma Woodhouse, and Dorothea Brooke, Gwendolen Harleth sees herself clearly for the first time during a period of deep personal adversity. Despite "that gnawing trouble in her consciousness" — that is, the recognition of the failure of her marriage — Gwendolen, the first sentence of this section tells the reader, at least attempts to appear happy. Sentences two and three continue this idea; Gwendolen has enough pride, at least, to resent pity.[31] And yet, as sentence four reminds the reader, she has become a mandatory resident of Grandcourt's "empire of fear".

Sentence five is the most important part of this section of the meditation. Gwendolen, the narrative voice says, has left behind her "girlish sauciness of superiority". What has replaced it is "an amazed perception of her former ignorance". Elizabeth Bennet never "knew" herself until Darcy's letter jolted her complacency; Emma Woodhouse never "knew" herself until she fancied Harriet and Mr. Knightley in love with each other; Dorothea Brooke never "knew" herself until she recognized the true nature of her marriage to Mr. Casaubon. And so the pattern is repeated. It takes error and the resulting despair to move into the light of self-knowledge and more objective vision. Gwendolen's revelation teaches her that she has misjudged Grandcourt and thus herself; her powers of perception have been faulty, mainly because her imaginative desires have led her to misinterpret outward facts. The same was true in Dorothea's case. Both heroines reason from wrong premises, from a view of things that has no basis in reality. For George Eliot, as I have suggested, a centrally important fact is the hard fixity of actuality, including most significantly the amount of will and intelligence a given person has in relation to the others around him. It is all, in sum, a deterministic picture of the dynamics of human life. And yet, as I have also been suggesting, the dynamic structures she defines are sometimes capable of undergoing reorganization.

Gwendolen has been blinded by the selfish egoism of subjective calculation. Grandcourt's "mental attitude . . . towards the woman he sought in marriage" is an attitude she never conceived to be possible, and this is why she suddenly realizes "her present ignorance as to what their life with each other might turn into". This is her "dread both definite and vague". She had examined the idea of marriage solely from a subjective standpoint before her marriage; her first concern throughout had been herself. And thus of course she failed to discern clearly the character of the man she married. If she did have a glimmering of the truth she managed to repress it beneath a painful load of personal concerns, concerns mostly soluble by marriage to Grandcourt.

The sixth sentence expresses eloquently Gwendolen's unenviable state of mind at this point. The "vague dread" of the preceding section and the "phantoms of the future" in this sentence both define the way in which the future exists for Gwendolen: it is something to be feared, to guard against, something that is infinitely more unsettling to think about than the "definite dread" of the present, which at least is known and need not constantly be anticipated. The seventh and last sentence contains some interesting diction. The reader is told that before her marriage Gwendolen saw Grandcourt "in the light of a creature such as she could understand and manage", but that since her marriage "Grandcourt had become a blank uncertainty to her". Once again Grandcourt is labelled a "creature" of sorts, and once again George Eliot seems to be playing off images of light and darkness against each other. She uses the cliché (ironically, perhaps) "in the light of" to describe what Gwendolen thought was her understanding of Grandcourt and the phrase "blank uncertainty" to define her present state of knowledge.[32] Yet Gwendolen's "blank uncertainty" represents a substantial increase in understanding over the darker period when she thought she saw Grandcourt in his true "light". Once again, the recognition of former ignorance is a necessary step toward a newly objective perception of one's self and the world. And finally, in this last sentence, the problem of the dynamics of will is raised again. Grandcourt will "do just what he will[s] ", and Gwendolen has no means either of determining or escaping that will. Her will is a physical force that is weaker than the physical force of Grandcourt's will, and thus of necessity she must be mastered by him.[33] Gwendolen's powerlessness in this regard is an analogue and a result of the determined nature of things in George Eliot's world, where contradictory energies constantly clash and where the strongest of the energies inevitably dominates.

Gwendolen, like Dorothea, is intelligent, and like her she reasons from erroneous premises. Both, also, remain fundamentally articulate during their mental crises. One of the ways in which they are different, however, lies in the makeup of their wills, that aspect of one's character that is so decisive an influence on one's life for George Eliot. Gwendolen's will is weaker than Dorothea's. Dorothea is able to confront her husband and even to resist him, as in the matter of Mr. Casaubon's testamentary conditions. But Gwendolen cannot resist her husband's strength. She is weaker. Dorothea is her husband's equal in the matter of will and Gwendolen simply is not. This is one of the major differences between them.

The meditation scenes in *Daniel Deronda*, like those in *Middlemarch*, seem to me to be central to the novel's overall thematic development. George Eliot's usual pattern of education emerges in her conception of Gwendolen's story, and it is precisely this process of acquiring moral vision which is rendered, at least in part, in these meditation scenes. Gwendolen's mind, as these scenes demonstrate, works in a series of self-blinding subterfuges before her marriage, and a bit more objectively afterwards. A corollary of her pre-marital blindness is the tendency to obfuscate issues, to vacillate, to rationalize. This is a function of the state of self-delusion, of self-absorption. Later, after her marriage, Gwendolen's rational faculties gain slightly more prominence as she begins to understand clearly and painfully the nature of her husband and thus her own former ignorance. The process of acquiring self-knowledge tangibly sharpens her perception in relation to others and permits her to achieve, by the end of the novel, a modicum of the sympathy that was so important to George Eliot here in this novel and in all of her others. One must look in to see out. Once again, self-revelation comes with sustained meditation.

Daniel Deronda is the history of two souls, Daniel's and Gwendolen's. I have ignored Daniel's story because it does not fit the general pattern I am attempting to isolate and elucidate in these novels. Gwendolen's "story" is that of her own psyche. In an essay entitled "The Natural History of German Life", George Eliot criticized Dickens for dealing only with the "external" aspects of his characters and said the novelist must deal with the "emotions". Here, as elsewhere, she does just that. Her realism is above all psychological realism.

Yet in the novels of both Jane Austen and George Eliot the minds of the characters, no matter how active or confused or how painstakingly observed, are constantly surrounded by the language of the narrator, which describes the mental action going on. The language of Jane Austen's narrator is often indistinguishable from that of the character, as a result of narrative effacement. George Eliot's narrative voice is more consistently its omniscient self and frequently emphasizes, in a number of ways, its detachment and separation from the protagonist of the novel. The narrator of *Daniel Deronda*, for example, often refers to Gwendolen with such epithets as "the young creature" and "the poor thing". The most striking difference, however, between Jane Austen's narrative voice and George Eliot's may be defined as something which George Eliot's narrator often does and which Jane Austen's never does. George Eliot wants the reader to see any moment in a protagonist's life not only as what it is in itself, but also in relation to all the other moments, in relation to all the other characters, and in relation to mankind in general. The narrative voice in her novels frequently guides the reader to this; there is no analogous phenomenon in Jane Austen's novels. Thus the irony inherent in George Eliot's narrative structure, while not so complex as Jane Austen's irony, is nevertheless virtually omnipresent. George Eliot's protagonists are of course unable to assess those other moments and those other characters as completely as the narrator. They are unable to see clearly, throughout most of the action, either themselves or the nature of their relationships to others. In a novel with omniscient narration, dramatic irony inevitably results. Sometimes this irony is difficult to locate, as when the narrator steps very close to the protagonist and puts himself in the position of a conductor of the mental energy going on. At other times, when the narrator stands farther away in order to point a general lesson, the irony is greater because the distance is greater. That is to say, it is at these times that the protagonist's ignorance is most sharply in relief. It is this fluctuating ironic distance between narrator and protagonist which most characterizes the narrative structure of George Eliot's novels.

George Eliot also differs from Jane Austen in her preference for dynamic or mechanical metaphors to describe the determined nature of human psychological activity. Her protagonists are no less intelligent than Jane Austen's; they differ primarily in being residents of a physically determined universe, in failing to see this, and thus in reasoning from inaccurate premises. Dorothea and Gwendolen are both intelligent and articulate during their mental convulsions, as are Elizabeth and Emma. But they have less insight into the nature of their universe, and therefore their imaginations, generated by egoism, interpret the world inaccurately. This determinism, which is both physical and psychological and which is emphasized throughout by the expression of human psychological life in terms of mechanical metaphors, is missing in *Pride and Prejudice* and *Emma*.

George Eliot's determinism of moral responsibility has long been recognized by her critics, and only the most naïve readers can claim that it is not there. Man, in George Eliot's system, must ultimately be partly responsible for his own actions because his character determines in some measure what those actions are. However, a man has only partial control over the nature of his own character; thus he is only one of the causes of what he becomes. A man's character is his fate; a man's fate, whatever it is, is therefore unavoidable and only partly determined by himself. It is all, in sum, a vast, abstract determinism, secular and physical. It is not, however, a totally immovable system, one in which man is incapable of amendment. On the contrary, if a man will attempt to improve or elevate those elements of his character that are destructive and selfish, he may very well succeed. These generalizations are usually accepted by most of George Eliot's readers. What is so often ignored, however, is her *psychological* determinism. Such an omission may be illustrated in one sentence which appears in an otherwise brilliant article by George Levine.[34] For George Eliot, says Professor Levine, "determinism is irrelevant in matters of human choice". I think we can see how inaccurate this statement is. George Eliot's fundamental determinism governs not only outward action but inner movement as well. Her determinism, as I have said, is psychological as well as physical, and this is why, "in matters of human choice", George Eliot describes the relations of conflicting forces within the mind in terms of unavoidable physical energies and mechanical balances. Some people, for her, are capable of choosing to be morally responsible, and some are not. And while it is of course desirable that men will will to do what experience has taught them is right, it is inevitable that some, because of their psychic make-up, will be unable to do so. Gwendolen, as we have seen, obfuscates the lessons of experience in her first meditation because of the dynamic overbalance in her mind of "imagination". The course of her mental activity at this point is just as "determined" as any physical action that occurs in *Daniel Deronda*. Later on she moves toward the acquisition of a modicum of moral responsibility, but throughout most of the novel the nature of her character prevents her from doing so. It is this psychological aspect of George Eliot's determinism that needs to be recognized. But the determined aspect of things, both physical and psychological, is for George Eliot no invitation to despair, as it perhaps is at times for Thomas Hardy; on the contrary, it is for her merely a part of the nature of things, a fact to be recognized and dealt with when possible rather than repressed or rationalized away.

And for George Eliot, finally, the epistemological relationship of a man and his world may vary and is dependent primarily upon the way he encounters that world. Her characters, at various times, encounter the outside world either metaphorically or directly — that is to say, sometimes they see it only in terms of, or as a reflection of, a private mental condition; and sometimes they encounter it so literally that it convulses their mental activity instead of stimulating it. Either epistemological situation is possible, and the question of which one shall predominate in any particular situation is decided primarily by the nature and perspicuity of the individual imagination in question. The most perspicacious imagination is that most purged of its originally generating force — that is, egoism. For the human imagination, for George Eliot, is generated by and results mostly from personal egoism, a particular form of blindness which often causes the individual to interpret outward facts incorrectly, to miss seeing them altogether, or to see what is not there at all. For her, one's "education" consists in large measure in the exorcism of an undue amount of imagination, which is often unreliable because of its genesis in egoism, and the cultivation of a more balanced, regulated, and rational view of the world, one generated less by imagination than by objectivity. The dissipation of self-absorption must precede the acquisition of sympathetic moral vision, and the latter is a necessary prerequisite for sentient and meaningful existence: this is George Eliot's highest aesthetic.

---

[1] For further and more detailed treatment of George Eliot's attitudes and theories about fiction, see her letters and essays and also R. Stang, *The Theory of the Novel in England 1850-1870* (1959), and B.J. Paris, *Experiments in Life: George Eliot's Quest for Values* (1965).

[2] Specifically, the best general studies of George Eliot's novels, in addition to that by Professor Paris cited above, are Reva Stump, *Movement and Vision in George*

Eliot's Novels (1959); Barbara Hardy, *The Novels of George Eliot: A Study in Form* (1959); and W.J. Harvey, *The Art of George Eliot (1961)*.

[3]See n.1, above.

[4]I shall deal with the problem of the two plots in *Daniel Deronda* later in the chapter.

[5]See n.2, above.

[6]See n.2, above.

[7]This is also the case in James's *The Portrait of A Lady*, in which Isabel and Osmond both misjudge each other. See my discussion in Chapter 5.

[8]*Middlemarch*, Vol.I, Chapter 20, pp. 267-273, *passim.*, in *The Works of George Eliot*, Cabinet Edition. This is the standard edition of George Eliot's works, and all further quotations both from *Middlemarch* and *Daniel Deronda* are from this edition. Between the first two sections of this meditation I have omitted a paragraph in which George Eliot's authorial voice comments to the effect that tragedy "lies in the very fact of frequency" and that the human frame can hardly bear much of it". These are the "general words" referred to in the second section. Between sections two and three I have omitted only a few words, and between sections three and four I have left out several paragraphs which recount a conversation between Dorothea and her husband and emphasize his "blank absence of interest in or sympathy" for her ardent desires.

[9]The architectural imagery here is similar in some ways to that used by Henry James in *The Golden Bowl*, and, to a lesser extent, in *The Portrait of A Lady*. The overriding difference is that here the buildings upon which Dorothea broods are real buildings, while in James's novels they exist only in the mind thinking of them. Nevertheless, both novelists use edifices — real or imaginary — and personal images of them to help define the state of mind of the character thinking. In Chapter 5, I shall discuss more fully both the question of George Eliot's "influence" upon James and his use of architectonic imagery. In connection with James's architectural metaphors, specifically in *The Portrait*, see the title essay in R.W. Stallman's *The Houses that James Built and Other Literary Studies* (1961).

[10]A similar process occurs, as I shall demonstrate, during Dorothea's second meditation upon her return to Lowick from her honeymoon.

[11]An interesting word in this section is "vista", for it is this word that James uses repeatedly in *The Portrait* to describe the process of Isabel's shrinking avenues of fulfillment. At the beginning of James's novel Isabel's vistas seem infinite, and by the end of it they are closed. George Eliot seems to be using the word rather more casually here, but she uses it once again, and it is undeniably appropriate to the suggestion of Dorothea's disillusionment expressed in this passage and again later on. Professor Charles R. Anderson first pointed this out to me in connection with *The Portrait*. See his essay, "Person, Place, and Thing in James's *The Portrait of a Lady*", in *Essays on American Literature*, ed. Clarence Gohdes (1967). See also my discussion of *The Portrait* in Chapter 5.

[12]What Dorothea is experiencing in this scene is very similar to what Jane Austen's heroines experienced in the novels I have already discussed, and is also similar to what Gwendolen Harleth and Isabel Archer will experience. It is in these last instances a case of disillusionment. In all five novels the woman misjudges the man, realizes her mistake, and begins to cultivate more carefully the art of vision that is so important to the writer who created her. The experiences of

Clara Middleton in *The Egoist* and Maggie Verver in *The Golden Bowl* are in many ways also similar, as I shall demonstrate.

[13]These generalizations will be further substantiated by Dorothea's second meditation and by both of Gwendolen's in *Daniel Deronda*.

[14]This passage is very similar to one in *The Golden Bowl*, wherein we see Maggie Verver "passing and re-passing along the corridor of her life." See Chapter 5.

[15]I shall discuss in detail the possible meanings of this pattern of imagery in connection with Dorothea's second meditation.

[16]*Middlemarch*, Volume II, Chapter 28, pp. 2-5, *passim*.

[17]This is exactly the same posture that Clara Middleton in *The Egoist* will adopt during parts of her meditation. See Chapter 4.

[18]George Eliot also uses the word "withering" in *Daniel Deronda* during Gwendolen's second meditation, which occurs after her marriage and the central theme of which is Gwendolen's disappointment in that marriage; and James uses the same word during the meditation scene in *The Portrait* when Isabel, in a similar situation, broods over the effect of marriage upon her "vistas".

[19]The parallels here to *The Portrait of A Lady* are obvious. See my discussion in Chapter 5.

[20]The same may be said of much of the language of *The Egoist*, *The Portrait of A Lady*, and *The Golden Bowl*. See Chapters 4 and 5.

[21]See *The Great Tradition*, pp. 79-125.

[22]Part of Leavis's discussion is devoted to proving that James's *Portrait* is based on *Daniel Deronda*, that Isabel and Osmond are Gwendolen and Grandcourt barely disguised, and that the Gwendolen half of George Eliot's novel is superior to anything in *The Portrait of A Lady*. For further discussion of these issues, see chapter 5, n.17, and the text of my discussion in the early pages of that chapter, wherein the question of the possible relationships between James's novel and both *Daniel Deronda* and *Middlemarch* is treated at some length.

[23]Daniel, incidentally, also has his meditations, the most striking example of which occurs in Volume III, Chapter 50, pp. 109-129, *passim*., as Professor Harvey also points out in *The Art of George Eliot*. I am not quoting it in the text of this discussion because it is not a part of the specific pattern I am concerned with here. The same may also be said for the "meditation" of thirteen-year-old Maggie Tulliver in Book 4, Chapter 3 of *The Mill on the Floss*, wherein Maggie "abandons egoism", to use George Eliot's phrase, after perusing such sections of Thomas à Kempis as this one: " 'On this sin, that a man inordinately loveth himself, almost all dependeth, whatsoever is thoroughly to be overcome;which evil being once overcome and subdued, there will presently ensue great peace and tranquillity' ".I think it is important to realize that other meditation passages do exist in these novels. The meditations I am examining as part of the particular pattern that interests me are not, in other words, thematically and stylistically unconnected with other parts of the novels; they are not idiosyncratic.

[24]*Daniel Deronda*, Volume II, Chapter 27, pp. 31-35, *passim*. Between the first and second sections of this meditation I have left out a few sentences which reconstruct part of Gwendolen's meeting with Mrs. Glasher. Between the second and third sections I have omitted two short paragraphs in which Gwendolen further rationalizes breaking her promise to Mrs. Glasher not to marry

Grandcourt.

[25] The yes-and-no, ebb-and-flow pattern here is very similar indeed to that of Daniel's meditation in Chapter 50, cited in n. 23, above, and it is, as I go on to suggest in the text of my discussion, a familiar phenomenon generally in George Eliot's descriptive language.

[26] The same, of course, is true of Willoughby in *The Egoist* in regard to Clara and of Osmond in *The Portrait* in regard to Isabel. More of this later.

[27] Volume II, Chapter 35, pp. 222-227, *passim*. Between sections one and two I have omitted a paragraph which reproduces the letter to Gwendolen Mrs. Glasher enclosed with Grandcourt's jewels. Between the second and third sections I have left out a paragraph establishing Grandcourt's knowledge of Gwendolen's broken promise to Mrs. Glasher and the further amount of leverage this gives him in his relationship with Gwendolen.

[28] The imagery here is also strikingly similar to that applied to Osmond by Isabel during the meditation scene in *The Portrait of A Lady*.

[29] Barbara Hardy deals with this aspect of Grandcourt's characterization in some detail in her excellent introduction to the Penguin paperback edition of *Daniel Deronda* (1967).

[30] Osmond is also described by Isabel in her meditation as the man who has "put the lights out one by one".

[31] The same may be said of Isabel Archer who, after her marriage, goes to so much pathetic (and fruitless) trouble to hide her unhappiness from Ralph Touchett.

[32] Once again I must refer to James's *Portrait*, where the image of the blank wall, the dead end, is frequently used to define the existence Isabel has unfortunately created for herself as a result of her marriage.

[33] The problem of the relative power of conflicting wills is also a subject that James is concerned with, but his treatment of it is not the same as George Eliot's. See my discussion of this issue in Chapter 5.

[34] See "Determinism and Responsibility in the Works of George Eliot ", *PMLA* (1962).

CHAPTER FOUR

GEORGE MEREDITH (1828-1909)

The works of George Meredith seem in recent years to have appropriated to themselves a rather casual air of controversy; there is little consensus as to his proper place among the English novelists. Like Hardy, Meredith was a serious novelist but primarily a poet who wrote novels partly to earn a living, and yet Meredith's poems, unlike Hardy's, are often neglected now, while his novels, both during his lifetime and since his death, have brought him both praise and abuse.

The two most common objections to Meredith's novels are those voiced by E.M. Forster and Virginia Woolf.[1] Forster, who finds Meredith the greatest plotter in English fiction, nevertheless also finds that he has not worn well — that he does not speak to us today.[2] He is, says Forster, boring and sentimental. Mrs. Woolf finds Meredith valuable as an innovator and experimenter, but her objection, which has been echoed many times, is to his didacticism. She feels that his characters always express one of his own views and are thus generally unreal. His philosophy, in short, is unassimilated, says Mrs. Woolf.

Meredith's later style has of course also contributed towards his relative decline in popularity. Forster calls it a fake, Mrs. Woolf calls it affected eccentricity, and many other twentieth-century readers have been baffled and disgusted by its convolutions and its preciousness. In many of Meredith's later novels, as in some of James's later novels, the major problem is a style of complexity and occasionally of affectation used to relate matters that are sometimes trivial (the famous banana-peel scene in *One of Our Conquerors* is an example), and the result often is an unintentionally mock-heroic tone. Meredith, like James, has to be approached slowly. One cannot begin with *The Amazing Marriage* or *The*

Wings of the Dove and yearn immediately for more.

Meredith, along with James, was attacked by critics in the 1880's for the wealth of psychological analysis he provided in his novels. Towards the end of his career, however, he was finally acknowledged a master psychologist of the novel. His method in most of his novels was to analyze the psychological texture of his characters and in this way to explain their actions. Since Meredith had an evolutionary view of character-development, it is not surprising to discover in his novels that, as the course of the author's psychological analysis advances, the characters are likely to change through a sort of organic growth. This helps explain the metaphors from physical nature Meredith often employs in dealing with his characters. Like George Eliot and James, Meredith believed that only by involving himself with other people in society does a person learn what he is. This process of learning in turn explains the evolution of personal change in his novels and suggests that Meredith too is deeply concerned with the "education" of his protagonists. *The Ordeal of Richard Feverel* (1859) is an account of the education of a Meredithian protagonist, and *The Egoist* (1879) is another. These, incidentally, are the only novels by Meredith still genuinely popular today.

Meredith believed that the novel should not merely be entertainment but should also teach people about themselves. (In this view he was by no means alone among the novelists of his era, but he was perhaps somewhat less successful than they at times in combining his philosophy and his art.) This is another reason why the theme of education — both of protagonists and readers — is a radical one in Meredith's books. The character learns from his own mistakes, and the reader in turn learns from the character's education. This, of course, is also the method of George Eliot. As her protagonists acquire objective sympathy, her readers are being educated to the necessity of human fellowship. In George Eliot's novels the educational process is that from egoism to despair to objectivity. In Meredith's it is that from animal egoism to rationality to love, or from blood to brain to spirit. Meredith believed that all sentient beings undergo this evolutionary process. These are the stages of Richard Feverel's development, and they are present as well in Clara Middleton's growth to maturity.

One of Meredith's most constant themes is what he calls the "comedy of egoism", and this also helps explain the dose or overdose of didacticism one is usually exposed to in his works. The "comedy of egoism" arises out of man's failure to perceive his place in the human hierarchy and his vision of himself at the center of the world.[3] As Meredith's own *Essay on Comedy* (1877) makes clear, the irrational man must be ridiculed, not tolerated. In this essay Meredith speaks of the value of laughter and the need for the perception of folly and "Olympian" mockery instead of sympathetic identification. What Meredith calls the "Comic Spirit" provides progress by deflating egoism and establishing in its place a sense of proportion. In *The Egoist* these doctrines reappear, and the ironic attitude of the Comic Spirit is maintained throughout.[4] Willoughby's main sin, like that of Sir Austin Feverel, is egoism, and in fact the theme of egoism and the need to conquer it, along with the theme of the loveless marriage, is typical of many of Meredith's poems and novels *(Modern Love, Beauchamp's Career,* and *The Egoist* are only three examples). These twin themes are also fundamental to *Middlemarch* and *Daniel Deronda.* Meredith was preoccupied, almost obsessed, with the phenomenon of egoism. One of his constant complaints is that people want, unreasonably, to *possess* others entirely. Among the egoists in *The Ordeal of Richard Feverel,* for example, Sir Austin is prominent for his desire to possess completely the heart and soul of his son. Richard's "ordeal" is his education, an education that advances him painfully and even tragically from a state of innocence to a state of experience. In *The Egoist,* Willoughby wants to possess his future wife completely. His egoism goes hand in hand with his inability to understand and appreciate the thoughts and desires of others, and this latter failing, as might be expected, leads directly to his downfall. His overthrow is inevitable because of his egoism.

Willoughby, however, is not the only egoist in *The Egoist.* As in other Meredith novels, most of the characters are guilty of the same sin. Even Clara, whose young mind is eager to grow in enjoyment and liberation, is an egoist of sorts. Her asceticism, like Dorothea Brooke's, is a form of selfishness.[5] But Clara is able to overcome both her egoism and her sentimentality through her love for Vernon Whitford, who must in turn overcome the egoism of his ascetic detachment.

Clara's education is constituted in her acceptance of Willoughby's proposal of marriage, her attempts to free herself from her commitment, and her final escape from him.[6] It is, like the education of most of Meredith's protagonists, an ordeal through experience. As Richard Stang points out, Meredith believed that the novel must affirm human freedom in the face of scientific determinism.[7] Meredith's protagonists, however, must usually survive some sort of imprisonment or incarceration before they can appreciate and learn to retain their hard-won freedom, and in this Meredith is once again similar to George Eliot.[8] Like *Pride and Prejudice, Emma, Middlemarch,* and *Daniel Deronda, The Egoist* is the story of a young woman's education, her progression from a state of blindness to one of objectivity and self-knowledge. And once again, the education of the heroine has its genesis in her relationship to the male protagonist and in the way that relationship changes or is perceived more clearly, at a later stage of education, by the heroine herself. That later stage of education becomes embodied, once again, in an elaborate retrospective meditation.

A major concern in succeeding pages is the language Meredith's narrator uses to describe human mental activity. For Meredith, a radical element of psychological movement is its flamelike rapidity. Thus his protagonists, once again intelligent and articulate, often think in terms of lightning-like flashes rather than in terms of balanced abstractions or conflicting vectors of energy. For Meredith, the act of thinking involves simultaneously all elements of the body — both mental and physical — and suggests an organic continuity between psychic and bodily activities. These facts help explain the prevalence in his novels of metaphors constructing analogies between human thought on the one hand and both fire and bodily activities on the other. Meredith, as I shall demonstrate, is somewhat less interested than George Eliot in commenting on the relation of his characters' minds to things outside of themselves. His primary interest seems to be in representing dramatically the organic movement of the human psyche, and thus his narrative voice detaches itself from the presumed inner voice of the protagonist less often than George Eliot's does. And yet the sustained wittiness and frequent sarcasm with which Meredith's narrative voice (an extension, as I have suggested, of the Comic Spirit itself) treats the thoughts of most of the characters suggests, once again, a demonstrable ironic distance between it and them. The distance between narrator and protagonist does not alter as often or as radically as it does in George Eliot's novels, but the ironic tone of the narrative voice prevails with some consistency, most particularly when the narrator is describing the direction and movement of Clara's imagination. The succeeding discussion will focus upon these issues, most of which are thrown into relief during Clara's climactic meditation.

II

The meditation in *The Egoist* occurs in a chapter entitled "Clara's Meditations". It represents an important segment of Clara Middleton's education — that is, a crucial stage in the process of her decision not to marry Sir Willoughby Patterne. Previously she had been docile, allowing herself to be persuaded by her sycophantic father and by the egoist himself that a marriage with Willoughby would tend toward her own happiness. At Patterne Hall, however, she is continually subjected to a number of cross-influences which begin to make her yearn for unconditional freedom. Finally, during an elaborate, lengthy, and agonizing retrospective meditation, Clara moves toward completing her "education" by beginning to see into her own nature (which requires freedom) and into Willoughby's as well (which requires possession). Clara, in a situation somewhat similar to Gwendolen Harleth's before her marriage, is infinitely more honest and realistic.

Her recognition of her cowardly feebleness brought the brood of fatalism.(1) What was the right of so miserable a creature as she to excite disturbance, let her fortunes be good or ill?(2) It would be quieter to float, kinder to everybody —Thank heaven for the chances of a short life!(3)

. . . Quick of sensation but not courageously resolved, she perceived how blunderingly she had acted.(4) For a punishment, it seemed to her that she who had not known her mind must learn to conquer her nature and submit.(5) She had accepted Willoughby; therefore she accepted him.(6) The fact became a matter of the past, past debating.(7)

In the abstract, this contemplation of circumstances went well.(8) A plain duty lay in her way.(9) And then a disembodied thought flew round her comparing her with Vernon to her discredit.(10) He had for years borne much that was distasteful to him for the purpose of studying and with his poor income helping the poorer than himself.(11) She dwelt on him in pity and envy; he had lived in this place, and so must she.(12) And he had not been dishonoured by his modesty; he had not failed of self-control, because he had a life within.(13) She was almost imagining she might imitate him when the clash of a sharp physical thought: 'The difference! The difference!' told her she was woman and never could submit.(14) Can a woman have an inner life apart from him she is yoked to?(15) She tried to nestle deep away in herself, in some corner where the abstract view had comforted her, to flee from thinking as her feminine blood directed.(16) It was a vain effort.(17) The difference, the cruel fate, the defencelessness of women, pursued her, strung her to wild horses' backs, tossed her on savage wastes.(18) In her case duty was shame; hence, it could not be broadly duty.(19) That intolerable difference proscribed the worst.(20)

But the fire of a brain burning high and kindling everything lit up herself against herself: Was one so volatile as she a person with a will?(21) Were they not a multitude of flitting wishes that she took for a will?(22) Was she . . . a person to make a stand on physical pride?(23) If she could yield her hand without reflection(as she conceived she had done, from incapacity to conceive herself doing it reflectively), was she much better than purchasable stuff that has nothing to say to the bargain?(24)

Furthermore, said her incandescent reason, she had not suspected such art of cunning in Willoughby.(25) Then might she not be deceived altogether — might she not have misread him?(26) Stronger than she had fancied, might he likewise be more estimable?(27) The world was favourable to him; he was prized by his friends.(28)

She reviewed him.(29) It was all in one flash.(30) It was not much less intentionally favourable than the world's review and that of his friends, but beginning with the idea of them, she recollected — heard Willoughby's voice pronouncing his opinion of his friends and the world, of Vernon Whitford and Colonel de Craye, for example, and of men and women.(31) An undefined agreement to have the same regard for him as his friends and the world, provided that he kept at the same distance from her, was the termination of this phase, occupying about a minute in time and reached through a series of intensely vivid pictures — his face, at her petition to be released, lowering behind them for a background and a comment.(32)

'I cannot! I cannot!' she cried aloud, and it struck her that her repulsion was a holy warning.(33) Better be graceless than a loathing wife, better appear inconsistent.(34) Why should she not appear such as she was?(35) . . . It is not possible to answer when the brain is raging like a pine-torch and the devouring illumination leaves not a spot of our nature covert.(36) The aspect of her weakness was unrelieved and frightened her back to her loathing.(37) From her loathing, as soon as her sensations had quickened to realize it, she was hurled on her weakness.(38) She was graceless, she was inconsistent, she was volatile, and she was unprincipled, she was worse than a prey to wickedness — capable of it, she was only waiting to be misled.(39) Nay, the idea of being misled suffused her with langour, for then the battle would be over and she a happy weed of the sea, no longer suffering those tugs at the roots but leaving it to the sea to heave and contend.(40) She would be like Constantia then, like her in her fortunes — never so brave, she feared.(41)

*   *   *   *   *   *   *

Clara looked at her thought and suddenly headed downward in a crimson gulf.(1)
She must have obtained absolution or else it was oblivion, below.(2) Soon after the plunge, her first object of meditation was Colonel de Craye.(3) She thought of him calmly; he seemed a refuge.(4) He was very nice; he was a holiday character.(5) His lithe figure, neat firm footing of the stag, swift, intelligent expression, and his ready frolicsomeness, pleasant humour, cordial temper, and his Irishry, whereon he was at liberty to play as on the emblem harp of the Isle, were soothing to think of.(6) The suspicion that she tricked herself with this calm observation of him was dismissed.(7) Issuing out of torture, her young nature eluded the irradiating brain, in search of refreshment, and she luxuriated at a feast in considering him — shower on a parched land that he was!(8) He spread new air abroad.(9) She had no reason to suppose he was not a good man; she could securely think of him.(10) Besides he was bound by his prospective office in support of his friend Willoughby to be quite harmless.(11) And besides (you are not to expect logical sequences) the showery refreshment in thinking of him lay in the sort of assurance it conveyed that the more she thought the less would he be likely to figure as an obnoxious official, that is, as the man to do by Willoughby at the altar what her father would, under the supposition, be doing by her.(12) Her mind reposed on Colonel de Craye.(13) . . . Even so little disarranged her meditations.(14)
She would have thought of Vernon, as her instinct of safety prompted, had not his exactions been excessive.(15) He proposed to help her with advice only.(16) She was to do everything for herself, do and dare everything, decide upon everything.(17) He told her flatly that so would she learn to know her own mind, and flatly that it was her penance.(18) She had gained nothing by breaking down and pouring herself out to him.(19) He would have her bring Willoughby and her father face to face, and be witness of their interview — herself the theme.(20) What alternative was there?(21) Obedience to the word she had pledged.(22)

He talked of patience, of self-examination and patience.(23) But all of her — she was all marked *urgent*.(24) This house was a cage, and the world — her brain was a cage until she could obtain her prospect of freedom.(25)

*   *   *   *   *   *   *

She went to her window to gaze at the first colour along the grey.(1) Small satisfaction came of gazing at that or at herself.(2) She shunned glass and sky.(3) One and the other stamped her as a slave in a frame.(4) . . . Her cry for freedom was a cry to be free to love.(5) She discovered it, half-shuddering: to love — oh, no, no shape of man, nor impalpable nature either — but to love unselfishness and helpfulness and planted strength in something.(6) Then, loving and being loved a little, what strength would be hers!(7) . . . If Willoughby were capable of truly loving!(8) For now the fire of her brain had sunk, and refuges and subterfuges were round about it.(9) . . . Were men when they were known like him she knew too well?(10) . . . She knew so much of one man, nothing of the rest; naturally she was curious.(11) Vernon might be sworn to be unlike.(12) But he was exceptional.(13) What of the other in the house?(14)9

Once again, nothing actually *happens* during this scene; Clara merely thinks, and in thinking clarifies her own perception, her vision of her own situation. She finally understands the folly of her acquiescence in Willoughby's marriage plans, and perceives, clearly for the first time, that she cannot survive without at least a modicum of personal freedom. She realizes that Willoughby's passion is that of possession and not of love, and in doing so she understands her own needs and desires for the first time. She too looks in to see out. Clara's meditation lasts all night, and it is a case of "incandescent reason", reason illuminated and motivated by feeling. Later on in the novel she decides definitively that she cannot marry Willoughby for the reasons she enumerates so rationally in this scene, and what the reader witnesses in the course of her meditation is the onset of doubt and the beginning of revelation. Clara's education begins with an increase in self-knowledge and objective perception, and culminates ultimately in her rejection of imprisonment with Willoughby in favor of the man she has come genuinely to love (Vernon Whitford).

Clara's sentiments at the beginning of her meditation are those of a helpless fatalism: Why not simply go along with whatever fate has willed? But sentence four proves to be the beginning of her self-discovery. Clara, "quick of sensation", now "perceived how blunderingly she had acted". The latter phrase reminds one of Elizabeth Bennet, Emma Woodhouse, Dorothea Brooke, and Gwendolen Harleth. It is crucial. Once again, the perception of past folly is a prerequisite of objectivity and clarity of perception, and this is precisely the "phase" (to use Meredith's own word) Clara is undergoing at the moment. She still seems to feel that she must acquiesce in the engagement to Willoughby, as sentences five, six, and seven tell the reader, but she has at least recognised the fact that she "had not known her mind". This is the beginning of revelation.

In sentence ten comes the first suggestion of the nature of *thought* as Meredith conceives of it in this novel: thought is something physical, something tangible, something one can actually feel. A thought of Vernon, says the narrative voice, "flew round" Clara; the image is obviously the narrator's rather than Clara's own. In sentences eleven and twelve Clara considers Vernon more closely. He is capable of maintaining his equilibrium, his self-control, because, as sentence thirteen tells the reader, he has "a life within". Sentence fourteen is also crucial. Clara thinks she might be able to imitate Vernon's stoicism; she is then assailed by "a sharp physical thought" and perceives, in a flash, that "she was a woman and never could submit". She is incapable of resigning herself to a life with Willoughby after all, particularly a sexual life, and she is just beginning to discover this element of her nature. The medium for the message is a sharp thought which seems to strike Clara physically and causes her to cry out, " 'The difference! The difference!' " Thought in Meredith's novels is something tangible, something material, something that actually causes physical pain and exultation. There is no evidence here, however, that Clara's own epistemological perspective, if indeed she has one, leads her to this conclusion; it is probable, as a matter of fact, that she is unaware of it. But that this is the view of Meredith's narrator is unmistakable;

he uses these metaphors several times in language describing Clara's thought-processes.

The discovery in sentence fourteen that she cannot be made to submit or yield to a possessive, domineering husband causes Clara to meditate further on her situation. "Can a woman have an inner life apart from him she is yoked to?" This may remind the reader of Gwendolen Harleth, who wonders about the ways husbands and wives think of each other, what the attitudes of married people toward each other are likely to be. Clara sees, in this section of the meditation, that if she were married to Willoughby his possessiveness might tend to deprive her of what she would want and need no matter whom she married — that is, a private, inner life, a life apart from and independent of her marriage. And thus, she concludes, a happy marriage with Willoughby would be impossible: he would want submission, and she "never could submit"

Sentence sixteen, in its suggestion of a continuity between thought and body, further emphasizes the narrator's conception of the physical aspects of the former. It also tells the reader that Clara is attempting "to flee from thinking", for she sees the direction toward which her thoughts are leading her. It is the direction of Constantia Durham, broken promises, disgrace. She can no longer look at the problem "abstractly"; her thoughts are too "physical". Her difficult position is imaged to her mind in explicitly sexual terms in sentence eighteen; if she is on the rack, it is the rack of her sex. In sentences nineteen and twenty the narrator sums up the problem: her "duty" would make her life "intolerable", thus what she has been considering as her duty must not be her duty after all.

The twenty-first sentence introduces a metaphor that will recur again and again in this meditation, and that is the metaphor of the "fire of a brain burning high and kindling everything". Thought is not only "physical"; it is now specifically compared to fire, having the same effects and causing the same results. It "burns", it "kindles", it "lights up" Clara "against herself". It illuminates her to herself. The phenomenon of thought being like fire seems tied to the ideas of volatility and personal freedom in this section of the meditation, which are themselves not wholly unrelated. "Was one so volatile as she a person with a will? Were they not a multitude of flitting wishes that she took for a will?" Fire is both uncontrollable and purifying, both unpredictable and emancipating. This is one reason why Meredith chooses this metaphor. It is a purgatorial fire; on the ashes of her self-absorption Clara will build a foundation for future vision. Sentence twenty-five repeats the fire metaphor in the phrase "incandescent reason". Reason, illuminated by feeling, is the fire, the light that will destroy the darkness of self-ignorance.

"She reviewed him. It was all in one flash". Clara's mind, usually rational, now begins to focus even more clearly. The fast-moving process of her revelation, expressed once again in terms of fire, is reflected in sentence thirty and is alluded to again in sentence thirty-two, where the narrator tells the reader that "this phase" of the foregoing meditative agony of Clara Middleton took only "about a minute in time" and was expressed "through a series of intensely vivid pictures".

In sentence thirty-three Clara finally and obviously rejects the idea of marriage to Willoughby. She feels she "cannot" marry him, and "it struck her" that her strong feeling ought to be a warning against the match once and for all. In the thirty-sixth sentence the fire metaphor recurs again. Neat answers are not easy "when the brain is raging like a pine-torch and the devouring illumination leaves not a spot of our nature covert". The fire of her brain, which seems to signal both volatility and freedom, is illuminating every corner of herself to herself. With the brilliant intensity of a forest fire, it leaves "no spot of nature covert", and thus Clara is seeing herself fully now for perhaps the first time. The "fire" illuminates every corner of her brain, and the onset of self-knowledge is at first distracting and agitating

Clara discovers that she will be unable to do her "duty", and the discovery, in sentence thirty-seven, "frightened her back to her loathing" of Willoughby. It is her engagement to him, known throughout the county, that will cause her disgrace. The fire begins to abate a bit, but "as soon as her sensations had quickened" her thoughts shift again, this time away from her loathing of Willoughby and instead to a consideration of her own "weakness" (sentence thirty-eight). Of the adjectives Clara applies to herself in the thirty-ninth sentence, the two most interesting are "inconsistent" and "volatile". She is indeed inconsistent, as her sentiments seem to be shifting constantly between revulsion for Willoughby and blame for herself. This is the basis of her "volatility". The imagery of the fortieth sentence explicitly suggests once again a continuity between body and thought, further emphasizing the physical nature of the latter.

At this particular wavering of the flame of thought it is self-blame that is dominant, and Clara, accusing herself of "only waiting to be misled" and exhausted by her mental struggle, finally seems to resolve, in the last sentence of this section of the meditation, to "be like Constantia" — that is, to jilt Willoughby, be the consequences what they may.

This first section of the meditation gives the reader substantial insight into the nature of the human mental processes as Meredith conceives of them. What distinguishes Clara's thought from that of the heroines of Jane Austen and George Eliot is its rapidity, its flowing, flamelike quality, and the union of reason and feeling ("incandescent reason") in her inner life. Elizabeth and Emma think in terms of balanced antitheses. Dorothea and Gwendolen think in a context of physical determinism, in which the human mind is pictured as a dynamic field of mechanical forces. Clara thinks not only logically and rationally, as they do, but also with lightning-like rapidity and total continuity. These qualities of her thought are reflected in the metaphors of fire throughout, to which I have alluded. Clara's thought is fluid, continuous, and organic. There is no distinction made between reason and feeling in her thought, a distinction made so often by George Eliot. Clara, unlike Gwendolen, is not pulled apart in many directions as she thinks; instead she thinks all at once. Everything in her thought is organically related to everything else. Even her body is involved in the process of thinking. All her feelings seem to operate instantaneously, and this is why her reason is described as "incandescent". The fire of Clara's brain is simultaneously a physical, mental, and emotional phenomenon; her mental activity, in the same way, is simultaneously that of feeling, reason, and thought. Only rarely does one see as clairvoyantly as Clara is described as seeing in the first section of this meditation. However, as I have suggested, Clara herself is probably unaware of the epistemological system suggested by these metaphorical patterns, which are a function of the narrator's language rather than of her own consciousness.

Meredith's narrator, though generally omnipresent and undeniably intrusive at times, is nevertheless sometimes disposed in this section of the meditation to efface his presence (as in sentences fifteen and thirty-four). Thus the language and its origin are occasionally ambiguous. The narrative presence never wholly disappears, and yet the narrator, in the process of reporting the activities of Clara's mind as he perceives them, seems at times to have his vocabulary and syntax colored in some way by that mind. In this he is somewhat more like Jane Austen's narrator than George Eliot's, for reasons I shall explain shortly. However, as readers we are usually aware of the narrator's surrounding consciousness; the wit with which the omniscient voice relates Clara's thoughts reminds us that Clara herself is not omniscient and invites us to view her from an ironic distance. The distance between ourselves and the protagonist is usually not as wide as it is in George Eliot's novels, however.

The opening of the second section of the meditation continues the idea of thought being physical; Clara "looks at her thought" and blushes, and the image is continued in sentences two and three. These three sentences, along with sentences sixteen and forty of the preceding section, suggest that for Meredith thought is not only something physical — it is explicitly incarnated in the body and in bodily gestures. In his interest in the bodily side of thinking and his suggestion that there is a constant continuity between body and mind, Meredith is patently different from Jane Austen and George Eliot. For him, as I have suggested, the activity of thinking involves all elements of one's being — both physical and mental — simultaneously. Once again, there is no evidence here to suggest that Clara herself is aware of these things. The narrator's language tells us more about his view of Clara's thinking than it tells us about Clara's own epistemology.

In sentence four Clara thinks of Colonel de Craye as a "refuge" from the pursuit of Willoughby and also from the agony of her own thoughts; he is now "her first object of meditation". In the seventh sentence it occurs to Clara that she may be tricking herself by idealizing de Craye, but this idea is instantly "dismissed" in favor of the more "soothing" mode of "observation" she is indulging in. Like Gwendolen Harleth, Clara will rationalize with little urging; unlike Gwendolen, however, she has enough sense to draw back from the precipice before it crumbles beneath her feet.

The eighth sentence brings the reader back to the metaphor of the "fire of the brain"; Clara is searching for relief from her "irradiating" — that is, inordinately active — brain, and thus de Craye now becomes a "shower on a parched land". There is for Clara "a feast in considering him"; he represents a pleasant digression from the difficulties inherent in her consideration of the engagement to Willoughby. The idea of de Craye as an oasis in the burning desert of her mind is continued in sentence nine: "He spread new air abroad". As Clara's mental "feast" continues, the imagery is repeated. In sentence twelve she labels thinking of de Craye a "showery refreshment" in the midst of adversity, and thus in sentence thirteen her mind is characterized as "reposing" on him; de Craye is the lake in the midst of the fire.

In dwelling so long on de Craye, Clara's "meditations" on the subject of her relationship to Willoughby have been "disarranged", as the fourteenth sentence reminds the reader. In the next three sentences Clara returns to Vernon's advice, his insistence in a scene preceding this one that she must make up her own mind about the engagement without anyone else's assistance. Vernon has told her that this is the only way she will ever "learn to know her own mind" (sentence eighteen), and that is precisely what she is in the process of doing. The "fire" of her brain is a purgatorial fire; it is ignorance of self and egoism that are being purged here, and self-knowledge that is being cultivated. The process of acquiring self-knowledge is not an easy one; it is, in fact, a form of "penance". Self-knowledge is a prerequisite for objective perception; this is what Vernon Whitford already knows, and it is what he is trying to teach Clara. One must know one's self before one can know the world, or at least see it objectively.

Sentence twenty-five, the last of this second section, is

particularly interesting. The imagery in it is virtually the same used in *Daniel Deronda* to describe Gwendolen's feeling of entrapment, and it is reminiscent in some ways too of Dorothea's second meditation in *Middlemarch*.[10] For Clara sees the house she is living in (Willoughby's) as a "cage" and herself as a prisoner in it; furthermore, "her brain was a cage until she could obtain her prospect of freedom". She has been imprisoned by the subjectivity of her own mind, by its egoism, its ignorance, its blindness — and also by the specific situation in which she now finds herself. Freedom, for her, will consist in an emancipation both from her own ignorance and from the entangling relationship with Willoughby. Freedom, then, results once again at least in part from self-knowledge and a concomitantly increased objectivity of perception. The art of vision, as in George Eliot's novels, comes with self-awareness, and until such self-awareness is a fact rather than a desire, Clara will continue to feel "caged". She is passing from the stage of egoism to that of reason, from that of "blood" to that of "brain". At the end of this section, then, Clara's self-discovery is still progressing; she has recognized the nature of her incarceration, and also what will be needed to escape from it. Her desire, above all, is for freedom.[11]

In this section of the meditation, once again, the source of the language one encounters is sometimes ambiguous (sentences nine, eleven, twenty-one, and twenty-three). The narrator's presence in these sentences is effaced sufficiently to make his voice indistinguishable from the thinking voice of the protagonist. The sentiments in these sentences are undeniably Clara's. Yet her thoughts come to us only through the medium of the narrator's surrounding presence, his own perception of the mind whose thoughts he is attempting to convey to the reader. Many of the verbs in this section are in the past tense and all of them are in the third person, and these things suggest that the narrative presence, while at times relatively transparent, never wholly disappears. The narrator is patently present, for example, in sentence twelve, wherein he comments to the reader parenthetically on the subject of Clara's thoughts. "You are not", the narrator says here, "to expect logical sequences". This aside emphasizes his

constant presence as well as his occasional separation and
and detachment from Clara. It also reminds the reader that
although Clara is thinking coherently, the sequence of her
thoughts follows a logic only of its own. Thus despite the
tendency of the narrative voice to become indistinguishable
at times from Clara's presumed inner voice, the reader can
usually locate the narrative presence because of its ironic
perspective on the novel's action. Sentence twelve is a good
example of this.

The first five sentences of the third and last section of the
meditation may remind the reader of Dorothea Brooke, who,
like Clara, gazes out of her window at a bleak prospect that
is parallel to the current state of her own fortunes. Dorothea
felt trapped, and the landscape in her meditation became for
the reader an emblem for the state of her mind. Here, too,
Clara stares at the greyness, getting "small satisfaction" from
"gazing at that or herself". Clara and the landscape are
explicitly linked. Both her reflection in the window and what
she sees beyond it "stamp her as a slave in a frame" (sentence
four), and thus she cries "for freedom" (sentence five). The
situation is similar to that of Dorothea's second meditation,
except that Clara, rather than dwelling at length on any
apparent contraction of the physical world as she views it,
turns immediately away from it to reason her way out of her
difficulties. Thus she does not experience her environment
as epistemologically as Dorothea does, nor does her experience
of her environment check the flow of her emotion or her
thought. The theme in this passage of freedom versus slavery
and the suggestion of imprisonment may also remind us of
Gwendolen's second meditation, where the concerns are
similar.[12]

Clara's "cry for freedom" is "a cry to be free to love", the
narrative voice tells us in sentence five. Clara is thus finally
discovering her own nature; which is that of freedom. She
must be free to love whom she chooses, and the climax of her
self-knowledge, her education, comes in sentence six: "She
discovered it".   This is the part of the meditation that
corresponds to the self-revelations of Elizabeth Bennet after
receiving Darcy's letter, Emma Woodhouse when Harriet
confesses her love for Mr. Knightley, Dorothea Brooke in

front of the miniature of Will Ladislaw's grandmother, and Gwendolen Harleth just after her marriage. The act of self-discovery is a tearing one; Clara "discover[s] it [that is, her own nature], half-shuddering . . . ."

Sentences nine and ten return to the metaphor of fire. "The fire of her brain had sunk", which means that the climax of her meditation has been passed and the agony of self-discovery is now on the wane. The waning of the fire also seems to signal the fact that the clarity of Clara's self-insight is beginning to pale and is now being replaced with some degree of self-deception. Clara has not as yet wholly escaped from her purgatory. This is why, in sentence nine, it is said that "the fire of her brain had refuges and subterfuges round about it". She knows that Willoughby is not "capable of truly loving", and any contrary opinion would be self-deception, pure and simple. Clara has finally understood that she must be free to live and to love, and this is another reason why the fire representing in part desire for freedom may burn lower. She is inching now toward the third stage of her development, toward "spirit", but she has not gotten there yet.

In the tenth sentence Clara wonders about Willoughby in much the same way that Gwendolen wonders about Grandcourt: Is he like other men? If not, how is he different? The last four sentences of the meditation tell the reader that Clara is "curious" about the nature of other men besides Willoughby, especially about Vernon and de Craye. It is clear here at the end that Clara will attempt as persistently as possible to avoid marrying Willoughby, which of course is exactly what happens. She escapes.

This final section of Clara's meditation offers, once again, several examples of narrative effacement and a resulting ambiguity of language (sentences six, eight, twelve, and fourteen). In other parts of this section the narrator is patently present, but, as a reading of the sentences I have just cited would show, he sometimes becomes more transparent. The narrator's language, in other words, sometimes becomes so colored by the sentiments in the mind of the protagonist as to render itself indistinguishable from the language Clara is presumably using to herself. I shall explain why shortly. In general, however, the narrator's

presence is intuitively obvious because of his ironic perspective
on the action and the constant wit with which he views
Clara's psychological thrashing, the outcome of which he of
course already knows. Nevertheless, the lightning rapidity of
Clara's intellectual movements seem to enable her, at least
part of the time, almost to keep pace with, or at least remain
close on the heels of, the narrator's (and therefore the
reader's) understanding of her situation, and there is thus less
dramatic irony here than in the novels by Jane Austen and
George Eliot previously examined, wherein the protagonists'
understanding is somewhat slower to come into focus — slower
in terms both of the passage of time and the velocity of
revelation.

III

The meditation in *The Egoist* seems to me to be of central
thematic importance in the novel. One of Meredith's major
targets for attack is the propensity of egoists to attempt to
possess other people, and he firmly believes that humanity in
its best moments can be free of this sort of tyranny. Thus
Clara's slow realization of her own nature — that is, that she
must be free (free, at any rate, to bind herself in love) — is
one of the novel's most crucial movements. She begins in
egoism and self-absorption, moves toward increased rationality
in her final objective viewing of Willoughby, and ultimately
frees herself to fall genuinely in love with Vernon Whitford.
The triad of blood, brain and spirit is just as apparent here as
George Eliot's triad of egoism, despair, and objective
fulfillment. The final Meredithian stage, that of love or spirit,
comes upon Clara later in the novel when, like Dorothea
Brooke, she recognizes that she has really been in love with
the right man all along. Thus Clara is another heroine who
must discover her own true nature, must see herself
objectively, before being able to view the world
knowledgeably. Here "the world" is represented by
Willoughby, and Clara's cultivation of the art of vision finally
enables her to see both herself and her world in its true shape.
She is another who begins in relative ignorance, suffers the
agonies of education, and emerges a more perceptive human
being.

The narrator's language during Clara's meditation, like the language in the meditations of Dorothea and Gwendolen, is often metaphorical. In the series of passages just examined the two most important images are those of thought as physical, and thought as fire. I have dwelt sufficiently on the possible meanings of these images. I would only point out that their presence indicates that in so far as the issue of figurative language is concerned, Meredith's narrator perceives the heroine in a manner more similar to George Eliot's narrator than to Jane Austen's. Meredith's style, of course, is essentially different from both of theirs, but in this matter he is obviously closer to George Eliot. Jane Austen's narrator, the reader may recall, usually does not use figurative language to describe the thoughts of the protagonists. He is more literal, more general.

And yet, the metaphors in George Eliot's meditation scenes and those in Meredith's seem to be present for different reasons. George Eliot's characters think in terms of analogies; this is evident in the language the narrator chooses in giving voice to their thoughts. Clara, as the narrator perceives her, does not think so often in terms of analogies. Rather, the metaphorical structure of her meditation results from the total continuity with which, according to the narrative voice, she thinks — a phenomenon expressible only in terms of metaphor. It cannot be described literally. Meredith, at least, does not try to describe it literally, but rather renders it dramatically through a series of images which keeps continually reappearing in the language the narrator chooses in giving expression to Clara's thoughts. Dorothea and Gwendolen think with metaphors because things get in the way of their perception, things often manufactured by themselves or by a lack in themselves, things which must be exorcised through analogy. The metaphors in their meditations also express, of course, the narrator's own view of the world in which they exist. The metaphors present in Clara's meditation exist more to render the nature of thought itself than to define the context in which it exists. They are more consistently examples of Meredith's philosophical expression of his idea of the human mind than they are functions of the fictional mind he has invented.

In the novels of all three writers — Jane Austen, George
Eliot, and George Meredith — the characters' minds are
usually surrounded by the omniscient consciousness of the
narrator's mind, and most of what the reader sees or hears
of the characters comes to him more or less indirectly
through that medium. In *The Egoist,* as in the novels of
Jane Austen, there are sometimes moments when the narrative
presence becomes transparent, the narrator's voice seems to
reflect the inner speech of the mind he is describing, and the
source of the words one reads becomes genuinely ambiguous.
In this matter Meredith is perhaps closer to Jane Austen than
to George Eliot. His narrative voice, like Jane Austen's,
sometimes becomes indistinguishable from the inner voice of
the protagonist as the narrator perceives it, whereas George
Eliot's narrative voice seems more often intrusively present
than either of theirs. This is because Meredith, unlike George
Eliot, is less interested in commenting on the relation of his
protagonist's mind to things outside of itself than in
demonstrating dramatically his idea of its organic continuity
and its startling rapidity of movement. And so he sometimes
allows the narrative presence to become partially effaced.
When he does so the reader encounters Clara's thoughts
more directly; their nature, as I have suggested, is such
that they must be dramatically represented rather than
described. Thus more ordinary omniscient commentary, such
as that in *Middlemarch* and *Daniel Deronda,* would be
insufficient in such circumstances. The human mind thinking
in terms of lightning-like flashes is for Meredith a phenomenon
that cannot be defined or evoked in conventional terms, and
thus he attributes to it the "incandescence" I have identified.
The mental processes, he seems to think, are virtually
supernatural, on a par almost with elemental energies. And
yet at the same time they paradoxically partake of the
natural, the physically human, the bodily. Thus they are
incapable of being expressed in abstract, descriptive prose —
as, for example, Jane Austen expresses them. For Meredith
there is instead an almost mystical sense of flashing lights,
breathless speed, and convulsive bodily responses. The
expression of this requires a narrator who will sometimes
efface his presence. Thus Meredith also differs from Jane

Austen in this: while the narrative ambiguity resulting from a partially effaced narrative presence serves in *Emma* as an ironic reinforcement of the protagonist's confusion, in *The Egoist* such narrative ambiguity results from the author's desire to represent dramatically to the reader the illumination of his maturing heroine. Genuine and total ambiguity of this sort cannot be sustained, given the generally ironic perspective the author has on his own heroine. But when this illumination is expressed it must be expressed dramatically — in terms neither of balanced antitheses nor of conflicting energies, but rather in terms of brilliant waves of light which illuminate the mind and the body simultaneously.

They also illuminate for us Meredith's imagination, the way in which he views the movements and power of the human mind. In his epistemological system there are few genuine interchanges between subject and object. Rather, the emphasis is on the incredible capacity of the human mind to turn away from what is outside of it (as when Clara cuts short her despondent gazing across the grounds of Sir Willoughby's estate, which seems momentarily like a prison to her) and instead to turn itself inward, away from all distractions. This, perhaps, is Meredith's definition of total rationality. For George Eliot, such turning inward is more often associated with the egoism of subjectivity. Self-discovery for her involves the act of seeing clearly both within and without. It is important that Meredith's heroine see beyond herself too, of course, but for him the crucial moment is that moment of turning inward to see one's self totally revealed, that moment of complete self-illumination which is a necessary prerequisite of moral vision. In George Eliot's epistemological system topography is sometimes an analogue of a mental condition. For Meredith the mind is its own place, and man can overpower topography with the blinding speed and completeness of total thought.

---

[1] See *Aspects of the Novel*, Chapter Five, and Mrs. Woolf's essay, "The Novels of George Meredith", written in 1928 and published in *The Second Common Reader* (1932).

[2] This is also the position taken by Dorothy Van Ghent in her essay on *The Egoist* in *The English Novel*, pp. 183-194. Mrs. Van Ghent, incidentally, also hypothesizes that Osmond in *The Portrait of A Lady* is derived from Meredith's Willoughby.

[3] See Ramon Fernandez's essay on Meredith entitled "The Message of Meredith" in *Messages*, trans. Montgomery Belgion, pp. 155-190. *Messages* was first published in 1927 and re-issued in 1964.

[4] This has often been noticed by critics. Lionel Stevenson's *The Ordeal of George Meredith* (1953) provides a good example.

[5] An excellent article on this subject is that by Irving Buchen, entitled "The Egoists in *The Egoist:* The Sensualists and the Ascetics", *NCF* (1964).

[6] W.F. Wright, in *Art and Substance in George Meredith* (1953), makes a similar point.

[7] See Chapter 3, n. 1.

[8] I would point out parenthetically here that he is also similar to Jane Austen and Henry James in another respect, and that is in believing that drama and narrative should be constantly alternated — that there should be few big "scenes", and that the novel's important ideas should be presented dramatically through the characters themselves.

[9] Volume I, Chapter XXI, pp. 238-245, *passim.*, in *The Works of George Meredith*, Memorial Edition. This is the standard edition of Meredith's works, of which volumes XIII and XIV are *The Egoist*. I have omitted two short sentences between sections one and two of the meditation, and just a few words between sections two and three.

[10] It is also practically identical to imagery in the meditation of Isabel Archer in James's *Portrait*. See Chapter 5.

[11] The same may be said for Isabel in *The Portrait of A Lady*, but the difference, of course, is that Meredith's heroine gets a second chance, a reprieve, while Isabel does not. James seems to feel that by the time one acquires the knowledge which is a concomitant of experience, it is, tragically enough, too late to put it to any constructive use. Such a theme is implicit in many of his other novels and stories, most notably, for example, in *The Ambassadors* (1903) and *The Beast in the Jungle* (1903). George Eliot and Meredith, on the other hand, seem more to feel that experience is merely part of the evolutionary process of human maturation, although it is of course true that in George Eliot's novels lack of experience is a frequent cause of personal tragedy (Hetty Sorrel in *Adam Bede* is the perfect example).

[12] Isabel Archer in *The Portrait* is also anticipated here. The question of freedom and the feeling of imprisonment are both central themes in her meditation scene. If Osmond is really derived from Meredith's Willoughby, as Mrs. Van Ghent suggests (see n. 2, above), then of course it is also entirely possible that Isabel herself may be a recasting of Clara Middleton. The situations of both, as well as those of Dorothea and Gwendolen in George Eliot's novels, are very similar, as I have been suggesting. I shall consider the problem of some of the possible sources of *The Portrait of A Lady* in Chapter 5.

CHAPTER FIVE

HENRY JAMES (1843 - 1916)

Let us suppose that a literature student, taking an examination, is given the following passage to identify:

The attachment, from which against honour, against feeling, against every better interest he had outwardly torn himself, now, when no longer allowable, governed every thought; and the connection, for the sake of which he had, with little scruple, left her sister to misery, was likely to prove a source of unhappiness to himself of a far more incurable nature.

The series of modifying phrases here, the multiplication, through grammatical devices, of linguistic discriminations, may possibly suggest to our student that the author is Henry James. The passage, however, appears in Book III, Chapter 8, of Jane Austen's *Sense and Sensibility,* published thirty-two years before James was born. Various experimental readers of this passage have attributed it to a number of different writers, one of whom, frequently, is in fact James. That one might mistake Jane Austen for James is an interesting phenomenon, for one is accustomed to hearing these days that Jane Austen is a writer rooted in the eighteenth century and that James is the father of the modern novel. They should not, theoretically, sound alike. But James was of course by no means the first novelist to concern himself with the possible intricacies involved in mirroring one's subject in one's style — in reflecting the subtleties of human thought in language sensitive to every pulsation of the brain. Similarly, his theories of fiction-writing, long considered revolutionary, were anticipated by some earlier critics and practitioners of the novel years before he published his famous essays and prefaces. Richard Stang, in *The Theory of the Novel in England 1850 - 1870,* has proven this very convincingly. The point here is that

116

James, like all writers, was influenced by preceding and contemporary authors. What is perhaps distinctive about James, however, is that he was not in many cases aware of how derivative his writing sometimes was. His obvious debts to Jane Austen, for example, some of which I have suggested in the introductory chapter of this study, are rarely acknowledged. He mentions her in an essay or two, sometimes with admiration — and that is all there is. The same principle holds true for the most part as far as James's gleanings from Dickens are concerned, gleanings obvious in *The Princess Casamassima* and *The Bostonians* but merely sublimated in James's writings into several nostalgic remembrances of the emotive effects of Dickens upon himself as a child and young man. When we come to James's connections with George Eliot, however, the pattern of unconscious indebtedness emerges in even greater relief. This is not to say that James was unaware of how important George Eliot's novels were to him; on the contrary, the large proportion of his critical writings devoted to her demonstrates how valuable an example he considered her. But he seems never to have realized the full extent of his indebtedness, and this can best be proven by considering the problem of the sources for *The Portrait of A Lady* (1881), James's first great novel and, along with *The Ambassadors, The Golden Bowl,* and *The Princess Casamassima,* among his best works. In my discussion of the sources of *The Portrait of A Lady* I shall also be somewhat concerned with James's possible connections with Meredith, and thus the question of *The Portrait's* origins is one that is particularly relevant to this study. While I have generally attempted throughout most of this study to avoid the thorny problems of "influence", *The Portrait*, because of its undeniable connections with novels I have already examined, presents a special case.

The crucial meditation scene in *The Portrait*, to be considered shortly, is similar in many ways to those of Dorothea Brooke, Gwendolen Harleth, and Clara Middleton, as my notes for preceding chapters have doubtless already indicated, and thus it would be difficult in any case to ignore *Middlemarch, Daniel Deronda,* and *The Egoist* in the course of any discussion of James's novel. The general situation of Isabel Archer, as well as the texture of her thoughts, bears many resemblances to those of preceding heroines, and thus I shall begin my consideration of James with a brief discussion of the possible connections between *The Portrait* and its three predecessors.

There is no doubt that James was extremely interested in George Eliot's novels. He wrote more pieces about her (essays, reviews, etc., totalling nine in number) than about any other writer.[1] The most important of these as far as any possible relationship between *Middlemarch* and *The Portrait* is concerned is James's review of *Middlemarch*, published in *The Galaxy* in March 1873. What is especially interesting here is James's summation in his own terms of the novel's story and characters, for it often sounds very much like what later became *The Portrait of A Lady*. Speaking of Dorothea Brooke, for example, James says: "An ardent young girl was to have been the central figure, a young girl framed for a larger moral life than circumstance often affords, yearning for a motive for sustained spiritual effort and only wasting her ardor and soiling her wings against the meanness of opportunity".[2] Such a statement could apply equally well to Isabel Archer, who craves the freedom to determine her own destiny and ruins her life in the process. She too is ardent, intelligent, and spiritual, yearning for the enrichment of experience, and she too is soiled by the meanness of opportunity. On the subject of Dorothea's marriage to Mr. Casaubon, James comments: "She marries enthusiastically a man whom she fancies a great thinker, and who turns out to be but an arid pedant. Here, indeed, is a disappointment with much of the dignity of tragedy; but the situation seems to us never to expand to its full capacity".[3] Isabel marries a man whom she fancies a great aesthete and who instead turns out to be a hypocrite and a prig. In this situation James saw the seeds of genuine tragedy and endeavored to expand Dorothea's story to its fullest tragic potential in *The Portrait*. On the subject of Mr. Casaubon, James notes that his "jealousy of his wife's relations" and his "hollow pretentiousness and mouldy egotism" make him singularly unattractive, and he concludes: "The whole portrait of Mr. Casaubon has an admirably sustained greyness of tone in which the shadows are never carried to the vulgar black of coarser artists. Every stroke contributes to the unwholesome, helplessly sinister expression".[4] Osmond in *The Portrait* is an undeniably different sort of man from Casaubon, but he too is jealous of his wife's relations, especially of Ralph Touchett; he too displays hollow pretentiousness and mouldy egotism; and the greyness of tone of his portrait also helps make him helplessly sinister.

Even if we did not have this review, obvious parallels between *Middlemarch* and *The Portrait of A Lady*, other than the ones already suggested, are discernible. Both Dorothea and Isabel, for example, discover the limited possibilities of a "larger life". And both, as George Levine points out, are disappointed in "an exalted passion; both accept their own limitations, their own unheroism, and the fact that they have made mistakes due to noble impulses".[5] Both Dorothea and Isabel are of a "Puritan strain", are of relatively good birth, have some money, and live with an uncle. Both are intelligent. And both, to quote Professor Levine again, "try to make their actions live up to the requirements of a large imagination which is consistently in conflict with possibilities actually open". In the Finale to *Middlemarch*, George Eliot comments to the effect that Dorothea's two marriages were the mixed result of young and noble impulses struggling amidst the imperfections of the social state; and in a Notebook entry for March 18, 1879, James says that the idea of *The Portrait* is that Isabel dreams "of freedom and nobleness" and "finds herself in reality ground in the very mill of the conventional".[6] There is an obvious similarity here. Also, Dorothea's rejection of Chettam and Isabel's of Warburton seem to be made for the same reason: marriage with these men would make life too "easy", too "predictable". Both heroines are highly theoretical and are constantly subjected to irony by their creators because they are so busy imposing theories on life that they are usually unable to read it correctly.[7] Despite the irony, however, both heroines are idealized to some extent and are meant to command the reader's sympathy.

Another major area of similarity between the two novels is that of their antagonists. Casaubon and Osmond are both dry, and the former's age becomes the latter's poverty in the transition from the earlier novel to the later one. The two heroines admire these men for their seeming lack of concern for wordly success and their supposedly good taste, and both women are deceived, disillusioned, and very much at fault for their own imperceptiveness. Both husbands are also inadvertently deceived by what they thought would be their wives' submissiveness after marriage. Casaubon and Osmond are both pictured as turning sour, withering, darkening everything they touch. Both are sensitive to public opinion while expressing disregard, and both are basically incapable of deep feeling of any sort. Dorothea and Isabel, Professor Levine points out, are both warned about their future husbands by men with whom they later communicate more fully (Ralph and Will), and both marriages fail due to conflicting personalities. The only major difference here is that Dorothea, like many of George Eliot's protagonists, gets a second chance for happiness, while Isabel, like most of James's heroes and heroines, does not.[8]

Finally, both George Eliot and James use Rome as a stage against which their heroine's sufferings can be given universality. But as Levine, Q.D. Leavis,[9] and several other critics have pointed out, James's Rome is a picturesque imitation of George Eliot's and not employed as effectively.

The case for the connections between *Daniel Deronda* and *The Portrait of A Lady* has been argued much more often and with at least an equal amount of persuasiveness by a galaxy of critics. As with *Middlemarch,* one may begin with James's own remarks on the preceding novel (published just five years before *The Portrait),* this time in the form not of a review but rather of a "Conversation". James's *"Daniel Deronda:* A Conversation" was published in 1876 in the *Atlantic,* and his comments on Gwendolen and Grandcourt, like those on Dorothea and Casaubon, could well be applied in many instances to Isabel and Osmond. James says:

Gwendolen is a masterpiece. She is known, felt, and presented psychologically, altogether in the grand manner . . . . And see how the girl is known inside out, how thoroughly she is felt and understood. It is the most *intelligent* thing in all George Eliot's writing, and that is saying much. It is so deep, so true, so complete, it holds such a wealth of psychological detail, it is more than masterly.[10]

In a subsequent comment on Gwendolen, James sounds as if he were specifically describing his own Isabel Archer:

Gwendolen is a perfect picture of youthfulness — its eagerness, its presumption, its preoccupation with itself, its vanity and silliness, its sense of its own absoluteness. But she is extremely intelligent and clever, and therefore tragedy *can* have a hold on her. Her conscience doesn't make the tragedy; that is an old story and, I think, a secondary form of suffering. It is the tragedy that makes her conscience, which then reacts upon it; and I can think of nothing more powerful than the way in which the growth of her conscience is traced, nothing more touching than the picture of its helpless maturity.[11]

Isabel, too, is eager, presumptuous, self-centered, vain, and silly, and she is also intelligent and therefore capable of undergoing genuinely tragic experience. The growth of a conscience into a helpless maturity — helpless because the maturity has come too late to save itself — is also the story of Isabel Archer. James's final comment on Gwendolen is perhaps the most convincing proof that he had her in mind when he created Isabel:

The universe forcing itself with a slow, inexorable pressure into a narrow, complacent, and yet after all extremely sensitive mind, and making it ache with the pain of the process — that is Gwendolen's story. And it becomes completely characteristic in that her supreme perception of the fact that the world is whirling past her is in the disappointment not of a base but of an exalted passion. The very chance to embrace what the author is so fond of calling a 'larger life' seems refused to her.[12]

Isabel, like Dorothea, is not as "narrow" as Gwendolen, but all three of them make the same discovery about the limited possibility of the "larger life", and all three are disappointed not in a "base" but in an "exalted passion". This theme of expansion is of course central to *The Portrait*, for it is the expansion of her intelligence and perception that Isabel seeks in her freedom and independence, and it is also the search for these things that, ironically enough, causes her tragedy.

On the subject of Grandcourt, James's comments recall Casaubon as well as anticipate Osmond. James calls Grandcourt "a consummate picture of English brutality refined and distilled . . . . I can imagine nothing more vivid than the sense we get of his absolutely clammy selfishness".[13] The phrase "clammy selfishness" also describes Osmond perfectly. And finally, James says that "in Grandcourt the type and the individual are so happily met: the type with its sense of the proprieties and the individual with his absence of all sense. He is the apotheosis of dryness, a human expression of the single idea of the perpendicular". [14] Certainly Osmond, like Casaubon, may be labelled "the apotheosis of dryness".

Also, in James's comments on the relationship between Gwendolen and Daniel, there is perhaps a hint, if one reverses the sexes, of the relationship between Ralph Touchett and Isabel: "It is a very interesting situation — that of a man with whom a beautiful woman in trouble falls in love and yet whose affections are so preoccupied that the most he can do for her in return is to enter kindly and sympathetically into her position, pity her, and talk to her". [15] In *The Portrait* the situation is that of a woman with whom a dying man falls in love and yet whose affections are so preoccupied that the most she can do for him is to enter kindly and sympathetically into his position, pity him, and talk to him.

A final connection between *The Portrait of A Lady* and *Daniel Deronda* specifically as well as George Eliot generally is James's preface to *The Portrait*. [16] In his preface, James comments that "The Isabel Archers, and even much smaller fry, insist on mattering. George Eliot has admirably noted it — 'In these frail vessels is borne onward through the ages the treasure of human affection' ". The passage James quotes is from *Daniel Deronda* and refers to Gwendolen. "In 'Romeo and Juliet' ", James continues, "Juliet has to be important, just as, in 'Adam Bede' and 'The Mill on the Floss' and 'Middlemarch' and 'Daniel Deronda', Hetty Sorrel and Maggie Tulliver and Rosamond Vincy and Gwendolen Harleth have to be . . . ." James refers to the "frail vessels" passage twice again in his preface; it obviously impressed him. He talks of "the difficulty of making George Eliot's 'frail vessel', if not the all-in-all for our attention, at least the clearest of the call"; and again: "The frail vessel, that charged with George Eliot's 'treasure' . . . has . . . possibilities of importance to itself, possibilities which permit of treatment and in fact peculiarly require it from the moment they are considered at all". Clearly, James's Isabel Archer was conceived at least in part out of the notion of those "frail vessels . . . of human affection" that George Eliot so often wrote about.[17]

There is no question, then, of there being a substantial connection between George Eliot and Henry James. He read her novels faithfully, wrote about them, and was obviously influenced by them. Thus it should not be surprising to discover that his heroines — and specifically Isabel Archer in *The Portrait of a Lady* and Maggie Verver in *The Golden Bowl* — bear some resemblances to George Eliot's heroines.

I know of no very strong proof that James was particularly influenced by *The Egoist*. His letters and essays rarely mention Meredith, and when they do Meredith is often condemned as boring. But James, at least, did read Meredith, and it is readily apparent that, coincidental though it may be, there is a basic similarity between Clara and Willoughby in *The Egoist* and Isabel and Osmond in *The Portrait*, as Mrs. Van Ghent has suggested.[18]   Clara, like Isabel, desires freedom and independence more than anything else. She too is a young lady without much experience but with intelligence and a desire to learn. A major difference between them, of course, is that Isabel's knowledge comes too late, as it usually does in James's novels, while Clara, like Dorothea Brooke, escapes a tragic fate.

Certainly Casaubon, Grandcourt, and Osmond are more like one another than any one of them is like Willoughby, but the radical element of all four of them is a selfish and brutal egoism. Willoughby Patterne is very much a part of this great tradition of egoists. He is not a scholar like Casaubon, but his dilettante interest in science bears some similarity to that gentleman's pseudo-professionalism; he has not the harsh strength of Grandcourt, but his possessiveness is not unlike that of George Eliot's antagonist; and he does not profess the aestheticism of Osmond, but his desire to possess totally everyone and everything is similar indeed to Osmond's mania for collecting *objets d'art* simply for the sake of self-gratification. Willoughby is perhaps less sinister in his strength than his predecessors, but that is only because Meredith continually heaps ridicule upon him; at base, he is not much different from them, and in his passion for

124 THE LANGUAGE OF MEDITATION

owning things he is specifically more like Osmond than he
is like any of the others.

What I have been suggesting is not that James is not
original, but rather that he was influenced by a particular
tradition in English fiction and that his own fiction would
have been impossible without such an influence. One can see,
in the passages quoted above, James reacting to a great writer
and appropriating what he wanted from her. And in the
specific parallels indicated in the introduction to this study,
in my notes for preceding chapters, and in the early pages of
this one, one can see as well a propensity to use not only
similar themes but also, on occasion, similar language. Yet
James was not merely a passive receptor of previous
literary achievement. He took the tradition of which he
became a part and molded it to his own uses, inevitably
altering that tradition in the process. In the remaining pages
of this chapter I intend to show not only how James was
similar to his illustrious predecessors, but how he was
essentially different from them as well.

My major thesis is that, for James, people constantly think
of things in terms of other things. They take relationships and
situations that could be recounted literally and instead
reconstruct out of them spatial scenes that can be dwelt on at
some length. His characters, again usually sensitive and
intelligent, pictorialize constantly. They have visions of
visions, images of ideas. They often tend to construct various
mental images of their own and circle around them, examining
them from every angle. These images are frequently expressed
in terms of architectural metaphors, which suggests that the
situations James's characters see themselves as being in are
basically of their own construction. These things are once
again most readily apparent in passages of sustained indirect
discourse and interior monologue, as we shall see.

II

The Portrait of A Lady, like most of James's novels, is written
in a style both metaphorical and indirect, for the typical
Jamesian metaphor here is that of an image of an idea, a vision

of a vision. Such a metaphorical structure stems from the usual situation of the characters themselves, a situation neatly epitomized in this remarkable passage from *What Maisie Knew* (1897): "If he had an idea at the back of his head she had also one in a recess as deep, and for a time, while they sat together, there was an extraordinary mute passage between her vision of this vision of his, his vision of her vision, and her vision of his vision of her vision".[19] James uses metaphors to define states of mind; he dramatizes pictorially conscious experiences, the states of the soul. Frequently the parade of images in his novels becomes symbolic of phases through which the soul of the protagonist passes. The "story" is often quite simply that of the characters' thoughts and is presented in a long series of images that play over the outspread expanse of mind and memory.

Everywhere, and specifically in "The Art of Fiction" (1884), James speaks of the "atmosphere" of the imaginative mind as a source for "hints of life. A psychological reason is", he says, "an object adorably pictorial. . . . There are few things more exciting to me . . . than a psychological reason".[20] James presumably means here that psychological phenomena easily lend themselves to metaphorical treatment, to translation into mental pictures. He makes another illuminating comment in an 1889 letter to the Deerfield Summer School: "There are no tendencies worth anything but to see the actual or the imaginative, which is just as visible, and to paint it".[21] The "imaginative", for James, is just as "visible" as the "actual". The "imaginative" transforms itself, for him, into the "visible", that is, into metaphor. This is why his representations of the human mind are pictorial and therefore so vivid and so effective.

James himself describes the elaborate meditation scene in *The Portrait of A Lady* as "the best thing in the book". Isabel's "motionlessly *seeing*", he says in his preface to the novel, is a "prime illustration of the general plan", by which he means that the heroine's education is the book's central thematic movement — a movement rendered for the most part through the dramatization of her consciousness.[22] Isabel's meditation takes up an entire chapter and is definitely a version of the general pattern I have been attempting to identify in previous chapters. It is a retrospective meditation, and its major focus is Osmond, Isabel's husband. In understanding him clearly for perhaps the first time, Isabel begins to perceive her own folly more fully and sees that she has been blind and self-preoccupied all along. Such new knowledge, while it cannot equip her completely to transform her circumstances, at least enables her to understand them. As in the scenes already examined, nothing actually *happens*. Isabel merely considers, "motionlessly sees" her husband and her own domestic situation.

To set the scene as briefly as possible — Isabel and Osmond are living in Rome, and they have been married long enough now for Isabel to see how completely she has misjudged her husband. They argue, in a preceding chapter, about whether or not it is proper for Isabel to visit her cousin Ralph Touchett, who is dying. Isabel tells Osmond that she will go despite his protestations. They part coldly, and Isabel sits by the dying fire far into the night, ruminating, like Dorothea Brooke and Gwendolen Harleth, upon the disaster of her marriage.

After he had gone she leaned back in her chair and closed her eyes; and for a long time, far into the night and still further, she sat in the still drawing-room, given up to her meditation.(1) . . . Her soul was haunted with terrors which crowded to the foreground of thought as quickly as a place was made for them.(2) . . . Her short interview with Osmond half an hour ago was a striking example of his faculty for making everything wither that he touched, spoiling everything for her that he looked at.(3) It was all very well to undertake to give him a proof of loyalty; the real fact was that the knowledge of his expecting a thing raised a presumption against it.(4) It was as if he had had the evil eye; as if his presence were a blight and his favour a misfortune.(5) Was the fault in himself, or only in the deep mistrust she had conceived for him?(6) This mistrust was now the clearest result of their short married life; a gulf had opened between them over which they looked at each other with eyes that were on either side a declaration of the deception suffered.(7) It was a strange opposition, of the like of which she had never dreamed — an opposition in which the vital principle of the one was a thing of contempt to the other.(8) It was not her fault — she had practised no deception; she had only admired and believed.(9) She had taken all the first steps in the purest confidence, and then she had suddenly found the infinite vista of a multiplied life to be a dark, narrow alley with a dead wall at the end.(10) Instead of leading her to the high places of happiness, from which the world would seem to lie below one, so that one could look down with a sense of exaltation and advantage, and judge and choose and pity, it led rather downward and earthward, into realms of restriction and depression where the sound of other lives, easier and freer, was heard as from above, and where it served to deepen the feeling of failure.(11) It was her deep distrust of her husband — this was what darkened the world. (12)

* * * * * * *

Suffering, with Isabel, was an active condition; it was not a chill, a stupor, a despair; it was a passion of thought, of speculation, of response to every pressure.(1) She flattered herself that she had kept her failing faith to herself, however, — that no one suspected it but Osmond.(2) Oh, he knew it, and there were times when she thought he enjoyed it.(3) It had come gradually — it was not till the first year of their life together, so admirably intimate at first, had closed that she had taken the alarm.(4) Then the shadows had begun to gather; it was as if Osmond deliberately, almost malignantly, had put the lights out one by one.(5) The dusk at first was vague and thin, and she could still see her way in it.(6) But it steadily deepened, and if now and again it had occasionally lifted there were certain corners of her prospect that were impenetrably black.(7) These shadows were not an emanation from her own mind: she was very sure of that; she had done her best to be just and temperate, to see only the truth.(8) They were a part, they were a kind of creation and consequence, of her husband's very presence.(9) . . . He was not changed; he had not disguised himself, during the year of his courtship, any more than she.(10) But she had seen only half his nature then, as one saw the disk of the moon when it was partly masked by the shadow of the earth.(11) She saw the full moon now — she saw the whole man.(12)

* * * * * * *

She could live it over again, the incredulous terror with which she had taken the measure of her dwelling.(1) Between those four walls she had lived ever since; they were to surround her for the rest of her life.(2) It was the house of darkness, the house of dumbness, the house of suffocation.(3) Osmond's beautiful mind gave it neither light nor air; Osmond's beautiful mind indeed seemed to peep down from a small high window and mock at her.(4) Of course it had not been physical suffering; for physical suffering there might have been a remedy.(5) She could come and go; she had her liberty; her husband was perfectly polite.(6) He took himself so seriously; it was something appalling.(7) Under all his culture, his cleverness, his amenity, under his good-nature, his facility, his knowledge of life, his egotism lay hidden like a serpent in a bank of flowers.(8) She had taken him seriously, but she had not taken him so seriously as that.(9) How could she — especially when she had known him better?(10) She was to think of him as he thought of himself — as the first gentleman in Europe.(11) . . . Isabel had an undefined conviction that to serve for another person than their proprietor traditions must be of a thoroughly superior kind; but she nevertheless assented to [Osmond's] intimation that she too must march to the stately music that floated down from unknown periods in her husband's past; she who of old had been so free of step, so desultory, so devious, so much the reverse of processional.(12) There were certain things they must do, a certain posture they must take, certain people they must know and not know.(13) When she saw this rigid system close about her, draped though it was in pictured tapestries, that sense of darkness and suffocation of which I have spoken took possession of her; she seemed shut up with an odour of mold and decay.(14) She had resisted of course; at first very humorously, ironically, tenderly; then, as the situation grew more serious, eagerly, passionately, pleadingly.(15) She had pleaded the cause of freedom, of doing as they chose, of not caring for the aspect and denomination of their life — the cause of other instincts and longings, of quite another ideal.(16)

*   *   *   *   *   *   *

The real offense, as she ultimately perceived, was her having a mind of her own at all.(1) Her mind was to be his — attached to his own like a small garden-plot to a deer-park.(2) He would rake the soil gently and water the flowers; he would weed the beds and gather an occasional nose-gay.(3) It would be a pretty piece of property for a proprietor already far-reaching.(4) . . . Nothing was a pleasure for her now; how could anything be a pleasure to a woman who knew that she had thrown away her life?(5) There was an everlasting weight on her heart — there was a livid light on everything.(6) . . . She lingered in the soundless saloon long after the fire had gone out.(7) There was no danger of her feeling the cold; she was in a fever.(8) She heard the small hours strike, and then the great ones, but her vigil took no heed of time.(9) Her mind, assailed by visions, was in a state of extraordinary activity, and her visions might as well come to her there, where she sat up to meet them, as on her pillow to make a mockery of rest.(10) As I have said, she believed she was not defiant, and what could be better proof of it than that she should linger there half the night . . . . (11) When the clock struck four she got up; she was going to bed at last, for the lamp had long since gone out and the candles burned down to their sockets.(12)[23]

The passages quoted above represent only a small fraction of Isabel's meditation. At the opening of her nocturnal vigil by the dying fire, the narrative voice makes it clear that her "motionlessly seeing" is strictly psychic vision — she closes her eyes and meditates. She is involved, says the narrator in a phrase not quoted above, in a process of "unexpected recognition", and her new insights will enable her, again in the narrator's phrase, to break "out of the labyrinth", to abrogate the prison of her former subjectivity and to see her marriage and thus her own situation as it really exists. It is, once again, clarity of perception that the heroine is cultivating.

In the second sentence of the opening section of the meditation comes the first suggestion of the texture and the pace of Isabel's mental processes — "terrors" crowd "to the foreground of thought" one after another. One of the distinguishing marks of Isabel's mind is that it is frequently "assailed by visions". The mind, as James conceives it, constantly incarnates itself in picture, constantly sees things in terms of symbolic representations of themselves. The third sentence introduces Osmond into the meditation; Isabel is "struck" with his "faculty for making everything wither that he touched, spoiling everything . . . ." The language here should recall the meditations in *Middlemarch* and *Daniel Deronda,* especially the latter, wherein Gwendolen attributes the same propensities to Grandcourt and also, as a matter of fact, uses the word "wither". Osmond's "presence" is "a blight", as is Grandcourt's for Gwendolen. Isabel is pictured in this part of the meditation as "conceiving mistrust" for her husband: "This mistrust was now the clearest result of their short married life . . . ." Such mutual feelings have become "a declaration of the deception suffered" on both sides (sentence seven), and Isabel sees a "gulf" opening up between her husband and herself. As in *Middlemarch,* each partner in the marriage has inadvertently deceived the other in regard to personality and basic character. And like Gwendolen Harleth, Isabel finds in her marriage "a strange opposition, of the like of which she had never dreamed . . . ." Isabel, too, finds it incredible that one of her husband's favorite occupations should be that of frustrating her desires, either directly or obliquely. And she has discovered that their values are different, a social theme that will be emphasized later on in this meditation.

The metaphor of the closed vista, so central to the meditations of George Eliot's heroines, now makes its appearance in Isabel's: "She had suddenly found the infinite vista of a multiplied life to be a dark, narrow alley with a dead wall at the end" [sentence ten]. James, like George Eliot, uses an image here of darkness and contraction as an emblem for his heroine's sudden realization of her past misjudgment and her present sense of imprisonment. "Instead of leading to the high places of happiness", says the narrative voice, using language similar to that of Dorothea's second meditation, in which the idea of "the clear heights where she had expected to walk in full communion" is introduced, Isabel's vista leads "downward and earthward, into realms of restriction and depression . . . ." The rest of the eleventh sentence, however, provides a point of departure from George Eliot. Isabel feels even the more depressed and restricted because, the reader is told, she has wanted to "look down" on and "pity" or "judge" others, like a goddess. This aspect of her character represents her flaw, her pride, her arrogance, her "bad faith". It is an aspect of character that Dorothea Brooke most certainly does not possess. Diminishing expectations and strangling realities are again expressed in terms of fading light as Isabel's perception and understanding of her situation begin to become focussed at the end of this section: "It was her deep distrust of her husband —this was what darkened the world".

Isabel, like the heroines of George Eliot, views her physical surroundings in terms of the contraction and darkness of her own expectations and experience of marriage. However, Isabel does not seem to experience her environment as literally, as epistemologically, as they do. That is to say, the imprisonment and oppression mentioned in the passage are less literal here than they are metaphorical, pictures Isabel uses to herself to describe her own feelings. The experience of her physical surroundings does not check the flow of her emotions; rather, it contributes to the "terrors" and "visions" bombarding her mind. The pictorial experience of contraction and darkness does not shatter her meditations; rather, such experience is incarnated into additional mental images for her own physical existence. Instead of being a product of literal or epistemological experience, these images exist for the most part as a result of the pictorializing propensity of the mind thinking of them. Isabel's mind constantly incarnates experience into picture — this is a radical element of the human psyche as James conceives it.

The narrator's language in this section of the meditation seems for the most part to be almost a transparent presentation of what is actually going on in Isabel's mind as he views it. The representation is at times so close that one might think that it could easily and without distortion be turned into first-person, present-tense rhetoric. Nevertheless, there are layers or strata in the language here, one strata coinciding with the quality of Isabel's mind, the other involving a witnessing distance from it (signalled in the past tense and third person) which expresses, it may be, as much the reader's spectatorship and distance as those of any narrator. The narrative voice reflects fairly directly what is going on in Isabel's mind, and its language sounds a good deal like her own inner speech as the narrator perceives it. It is all, in sum, the narrator's closely sympathetic account of the protagonist's impressions, to anticipate a phrase James uses in connection with *The Golden Bowl.* Isabel's inner speech is reported to the reader by the narrative voice as directly as possible and is altered only insofar as it is expressed in grammatical English. The narrator's "account" is necessary for selection and organization, for distance and objectivity. His is a cool, effacing presence — one which usually eschews generalization and universal moralizing.

Isabel's "active condition" of "suffering" is described by the narrator at the opening of the second section of the meditation not as something cold and passive but rather as "a passion of thought, of speculation, of response to every pressure". This is the way Isabel thinks, the way her mind works — rapidly, passionately, even at times frenziedly. Hers is "a passion of thought, of speculation", and the text mirrors pretty exactly the texture of her mind. The narrative presence seems momentarily more in evidence here as the reader encounters these comments, but then there is a return to something more intimate, more ambiguous, as the passage continues. Much of it, once again, could with little distortion be transformed into first-person, present-tense constructions were not the narrator's presence necessary to preserve coherence.

The fifth sentence of this second section picks up again the image of fading light so important in the meditations in George Eliot's novels and already reintroduced in the first section of this one: "the shadows had begun to gather; it was as if Osmond deliberately, almost malignantly, had put the lights out one by one". This is very similar to Gwendolen's second meditation, and suggestive to some extent too of Dorothea's reaction to Mr. Casaubon. In all three cases the imagery suggests the contraction and the muffling of expectations in a shroud of disappointment and disillusionment. For George Eliot's heroines the darkness was literal, a result of the way they actually experienced their environments after their marriages. For Clara Middleton, the feeling of imprisonment could be reasoned out of existence. For Isabel, the darkness exists primarily in the mental image she has of it. Her mind works in terms of visions and images of things, and the image of darkness, of contraction, is present to her in various pictorial representations of it throughout most of her meditation. She frequently connects her husband with her vision of darkness, as in the sentence quoted above and again in sentences six and seven of this section: "The dusk was at first vague and thin, and she could still see her way in it. But it steadily deepened, and if now and again it had occasionally lifted there were certain corners of her prospect that were impenetrably black". Physical darkness becomes here a metaphor for the coercive effect of Osmond's personality. Isabel views the effects of his personality on her own in terms of changing spheres of light and darkness. She sees things, typically, in terms of other things. The "shadows" preoccupying Isabel are once again seen as a direct emanation of Osmond himself in sentence nine. Grandcourt, it may be recalled, is constantly associated by Gwendolen with darkness and by the narrative voice, later on, with Satan himself. Gwendolen, however, saw her husband as literally dark, as a truly Satanic "creature", while Isabel sees her husband in terms of a mental image of him that exists only in her own mind. She experiences his presence metaphorically rather than physically.

Isabel's central revelation takes place in the last part of this section of the meditation, and it is a revelation expressed once again in terms of darkness and light. It is not that Osmond is any different. Isabel's mental image of him is different. Isabel sees that it is she herself who has changed, a change resulting from increased clarity of perception. She now *sees* differently. Like Dorothea in front of Aunt Julia's portrait, it is the beholder whose perception changes rather than the object of perception itself. Osmond is the same, but before her marriage, like Dorothea before hers, "she had seen only half his nature . . . as one saw the disk of the moon when it was partly masked by the shadow of the earth. She saw the full moon now — she saw the whole man". Here is the crux of Isabel's revelation. She has not really known her husband until now, which means that she had misjudged him before. He is not what she thought — like Elizabeth Bennet, she has been wrong all along. Part of Osmond's nature, like the disk of the moon, had been shrouded in the shadow of her own ignorance; it had always been there, but she had been unable to see it. Now the darkness of ignorance fades before the light of discovery, and Osmond's character and Isabel's own blindness both stand totally revealed. This is a crucial moment in Isabel's vigil. For her, as for Maggie in *The Golden Bowl*, the confrontation of and insight into a situation tends to embody itself in a picture which is a spatial scene that can be brooded on. These mental images reconstruct a scene or a situation that could be treated in a straightforward (that is, unmetaphorical) way. But James's protagonists see things in terms of other things, analogically, and thus their thoughts are frequently expressed in terms of images such as the one just examined. As in George Eliot's novels, the language plays off light and darkness against each other to express the process of self-discovery that is going on within the protagonist. Out of the darkness comes the light of new knowledge, self-knowledge, and concomitantly increased clarity of perception. This is the moment when Isabel's mistake in judgment becomes manifestly present to her, and as such it has obvious thematic connections with the meditations examined in preceding chapters. Most of her revelation is related to the reader in the third-person and past-tense constructions of the narrative voice (usually, as in Elizabeth Bennet's meditation, "She saw").

The third section of the meditation introduces another image common to some of the meditations examined previously. Like George Eliot's heroines and, even more specifically, like Clara Middleton, Isabel sees herself as imprisoned in the house in which she is living. Unlike Clara, however, Isabel is unable to turn away from her surroundings and reason her way out of her "prison". The prison exists as an image within her own mind, and it stays with her. She feels, in keeping with the imagery of previous passages, that she is existing in the midst of darkness and suffocation. Osmond's presence seems to deny her light and air. The narrator's language emphasizes the fact that the imprisonment is a moral, or a mental, imprisonment. "She could come and go", and Osmond's oppressiveness is not physical. The idea of imprisonment is a result of Isabel's vision of a vision of herself. Osmond is polite to her, yet beneath his polished exterior, Isabel now discovers, "his egotism lay hidden like a serpent in a bank of flowers" [sentence eight]. Here the imagery is like that Gwendolen and the narrator of *Daniel Deronda* apply to Grandcourt. Osmond's diabolical pride and passion for possession, like Grandcourt's (and Willoughby's), are personality factors no less radical to his nature simply because they are somewhat obscured by his polished manners and his social graces. He is still a devil.

Isabel's rediscovery of her moral restriction continues in sentence twelve in the image of her being required by Osmond to "march to the stately music" of his past. Like Clara Middleton, it is the loss of her prized freedom that makes Isabel feel so constricted. She is no longer "so free of step"; there are "certain things they must do". In sentence fourteen this same cluster of images is repeated; as this "rigid system" closes about her, a "sense of darkness and suffocation" comes over her, and she seems to herself to be "shut up with an odour of mold and decay". In his review of *Middlemarch*, it may be recalled, James used the phrase "mouldy egotism" in discussing Casaubon, and Isabel's feelings about her husband in this section of the meditation are remarkably similar to Dorothea's. A major difference between the novels, however, seems to lie in the emphasis here on the way in which Osmond incarnates a *social* coercion, a rigid system of acting and behaving. Isabel's shrinking away from her husband results, in other words, primarily from the coercive effect of Osmond's personality on her own. One may distinguish this meditation from those examined previously at least in part through its emphasis on a coercive social system that tends literally and physically to restrict one if one permits it to do so. Such a theme, of course, is one with which readers of James should be familiar.[24] The topographical contraction here, then, is not only metaphorical (an image in Isabel's mind) but also literal and real. Isabel is restricted from doing or saying certain things because of her husband's prohibitions. From this literal oppression she seems to extrapolate, however, a further metaphorical oppression which is expressed in the image of suffocation, a metaphorical closeting with the odors of mold and decay.

Isabel's sense of imprisonment brings with it that feeling of constriction and strangulation we have already encountered in previous meditations. Her misjudgment, her mismarriage, enlighten her on the subject of her own former ignorance, and she feels trapped until her way is cleared somewhat by a more perceptive understanding of her position in regard to others, especially in regard to her husband. Isabel, the reader is told, "had resisted" this process of incarceration. Like Clara, she had "pleaded the cause of freedom, of doing as they chose, of not caring for the aspect and denomination of their life". Like Clara's, her pleading has failed; but, unlike Clara, she has no avenue of escape, as the language of this section makes clear. Nevertheless, Isabel is by no means totally defeated, as Gwendolen was. She resists Osmond. In this context the question of opposed wills is raised once again.[25] In George Eliot's novels the conflict of wills was part of the determined nature of things. The conclusion was always foregone, the stronger will triumphing every time. Grandcourt dominates Gwendolen because he is stronger than she is. Casaubon, finally, is unable to master Dorothea because he is *not* stronger than she is. But in *The Portrait,* as well as in *The Golden Bowl,* the clash of wills often has a more unpredictable conclusion. It is not inevitable in James's novels that the stronger will triumphs over the weaker. Rather, the weaker person is often able, through evasiveness or strategy of some kind, at least to hold his own. Isabel "loses" in the sense that her life has been ruined by her husband, but he is nevertheless unable to dominate her as completely as Grandcourt dominates Gwendolen. Gwendolen would not visit a sick cousin if her husband forbade it. Isabel, like Maggie Verver in *The Golden Bowl,* essentially "wins" by losing, or in the process of losing. Her husband is never able to control her totally. James, then, took a theme that was one of George Eliot's constant concerns and changed it to fit his own designs. And in doing so, he perhaps gives the lie to those of his students who claim that he never had an idea in his life. Certainly it is true that James does not write "thesis" novels in the style of Mrs. Gaskell or the later Wilkie Collins. His opinions on such matters as religion, politics, economics, and metaphysics are doubtless difficult to discern, and perhaps non-existent after all. But James, as everyone knows, was an avid philosopher of human nature, a painstaking observer of the personal relations and behavior of our species, and of course he always demonstrates this in a thousand ways. In his view of human interpersonal relations he is obviously quite different from George Eliot. For the latter, the nature and the results of human relationships are fixed according to the make-up of the human beings involved. Character is fate, and neither can change the other without great exertion. But for James, human relationships seem more fluid, more unpredictable, capable of changing balance at any moment. He believed strongly that people should act as if free will were a fact instead of merely a possibility. Thus his weak people are often indomitable in some way, while his strong people are sometimes unable to domineer. Such a view of humanity, as in the novels of Dostoevski, helps sustain our interest in the protagonists, for there is always the fascinating possibility that a character may act at variance with what we have come to consider his "nature". And such is the reality of human life. "Round" characters *are* inconsistent; it is only the one-dimensional characters of fiction who are totally predictable.

James makes it quite clear in this third section of the meditation that his narrator, though often transparent, is a virtually omnipresent entity. In sentence fourteen, summing up Isabel's feelings of restriction, the narrative voice says that "that sense of darkness and suffocation of which I have spoken took possession of her . . . ." The first-person pronoun makes it obvious that the narrative presence, though at times self-effacing and relatively unobtrusive, never wholly disappears. That presence is a necessary medium for the conveyance of Isabel's "passion" and "suffering". Her suffering is not "physical", the reader is told. She is undergoing a mental convulsion, which is communicated to the reader as seen through the all-surrounding mind of the narrator.

In the fourth and last section of the meditation, Isabel sees clearly what it is about her that has offended and alienated her husband; it is her desire for freedom, both personal and psychological. The garden metaphor of the first four sentences tells the reader that Isabel thinks that Osmond, in his passion for ownership, wants to own her mind as well as the rest of her. It is precisely this aspect of Willoughby that Clara Middleton rebels against. Clara too feels the need for an "inner life" apart from anyone else. The garden metaphor, however, is somewhat anomalous. It is certainly less coherent than Isabel's previous mental images of the clash of wills, Osmond's and hers, of the pressure of conflicting personalities. Such an impalpable phenomenon is made concrete first in one metaphor and then in another, for the metaphors here are usually "as ifs", fictions within the larger fiction of the novel, transfers from one realm of fictive language into another, and indirect revelations of the fact that Isabel and Osmond, like all fictional characters, exist only as the language of the novel presents them to the reader.

The fifth sentence states the central lesson of Isabel's meditation: she has thrown her life away. There is no escape for her. Unlike Dorothea and Clara, Isabel will receive no reprieve. By the time the fruits of experience are gathered, it is too late to make use of them. Thus there is "an everlasting weight on her heart" and "a livid light on everything". The darkness of restriction and ignorance is ironically dissipating in the path of the light of Isabel's new and tragic knowledge. And this is why the light is "livid", hopeless, heartbreaking.

The last half of this section sums up for the reader once again Isabel's state of mind. She is "in a fever" and takes "no heed of time". For Clara Middleton, the passage of time was important, for she was constantly concerned with the problem of how to live her life. Time, however, cannot matter to Isabel. For her, time does not pass. She is trapped, her life is over, time is no more. Her mind, says the narrator, "assailed by visions, was in a state of extraordinary activity". Once again, this is a key to understanding how the human mind works for James. It is continuously "assailed by visions", and the result is a series of intensely vivid pictures that serves to reconstruct literal scenes in terms of personal images of them.

When Isabel finally goes off to bed it is through the physical darkness of the lampless and candleless rooms.

Whatever light she requires she must provide from within.

In this section of Isabel's meditation the narrator again is sometimes self-effacing (sentences three and four), and thus the reader seems occasionally to hear Isabel's thoughts directly, without intermediary. Jane Austen's narrator often effaced his presence in order to mirror the ironic confusion of the protagonist's mind. Meredith's narrator sometimes disappeared from view so that the rhythms of Clara's mental processes could be rendered dramatically. James's narrator also becomes transparent on occasion, and when this happens it seems to be because James wants the reader to see the image-generating propensities of Isabel's mind, a phenomenon which, like the lightning-flashes of Clara's mental processes, cannot be described but rather must be shown in full flight.

The language of this final section generally reflects or transmits the "extraordinary activity" of Isabel's mind. She has "ultimately perceived" what it is about herself that offends Osmond (it is her desire for freedom from his influence), and sentences eight, nine, and ten emphasize the fevered nature of her cogitation, the rapid movement of a mind "assailed by visions". The phrase "As I have said" in sentence eleven reminds the reader once again, however, that the narrative presence never wholly disappears; what the reader receives is the narrator's report of Isabel's inner speech as he perceives it.

Like the heroines of Jane Austen, George Eliot, and George Meredith, James's protagonist is intelligent and articulate and continues to think logically during her period of mental convulsion. Unlike Jane Austen's heroines, however, and like those of George Eliot and Meredith, Isabel thinks less in terms of abstract generalizations than in terms of mental pictures, images remarkably similar to some of those also employed by the two preceding writers. James's characters, in other words, frequently think of things in terms of other things, and in this they are unlike Jane Austen's characters, who are more literal. But Isabel is not pictured as thinking in a mechanistic context of the clash of physical energies, and her thoughts also seem to be more "feverish" than those of Dorothea and Gwendolen. In this latter respect, perhaps, she is more like Clara Middleton. Unlike Clara, however,

Isabel does not think with all of her energies, both mental and physical, simultaneously. What seems to be unique about her mind is its tendency to take a scene or a relationship or a situation of some kind that could be recounted in literal language and reconstruct it mentally into a metaphor of itself. Isabel, as I have said, constantly sees things in terms of other things. Her visions are visions of visions, images of ideas. Her mental processes, though extraordinarily active, are relatively more static than Clara's. James's protagonists, in *The Golden Bowl* as well as in *The Portrait*, tend to construct various mental images of their own and then circle around them, as it were, examining them from every possible angle. The images themselves, in other words, are relatively stationary. In *The Egoist* the feeling one gets during Clara's meditation is that of constant and rapid movement (as that of fire, for example) — less a situation of stasis than one of flashing and instantaneous change.

Like George Eliot's narrator, James's is capable both of sympathetic identification with the protagonist and of cool detachment from her. Yet James's narrative voice does not use the periods of its relative detachment to draw universal morals, and this is one reason why the narrator's language becomes more often indistinguishable from the protagonist's presumed inner speech in *The Portrait* than in either *Middlemarch* or *Daniel Deronda*. In this respect, James's narrator is perhaps more like Jane Austen's and Meredith's. In his insistence that he is merely giving the reader an "account" of an "impression", however, he is essentially different from all of the others. James makes this statement, as I have said, specifically in connection with the narrative technique of *The Golden Bowl*, but it is also the technique of *The Portrait of A Lady* — a technique both metaphorical and indirect, emphasizing the pictorializing tendencies of the human mind.

The meditation scene in *The Portrait*, like those in preceding novels already examined, is a pivotal one in the novel's thematic progression. In her meditation Isabel, like her predecessors, motionlessly sees, through her realization of Osmond's real nature, how blind she herself has been. Her altered perspective on her husband, like Dorothea's and

Gwendolen's, makes her more aware of her former ignorance and her present situation. The meditation represents, once again, a lapsing of the dramatic irony inherent in the failure of her comprehension of things to keep pace with that of the narrator (and through him with that of the reader). What Isabel has jealously guarded all through the novel is her independence; and it was to help preserve that independence that old Mr. Touchett, at Ralph's urging, left her a fortune. Ralph wanted to see what Isabel would do with complete liberty. What she does is to prove that freedom and independence without experience and understanding are a catastrophic combination, a typically Jamesian theme. What she learns, tragically enough, is that she has learned too late. Her life has been ruined.

III

The Golden Bowl (1904), like The Portrait of A Lady, is written in a style both metaphorical and indirect, for once again the usual metaphor in the novel is that of an image of an idea, a vision of a vision. In The Golden Bowl, however, the metaphors tend more often to be architectural images, and it is on this pattern that I shall concentrate in my discussion of the novel.[26] James uses variations of the metaphor consistently in this novel when dealing with the human psyche, and an examination of its meaning should further help to define the nature of the human mental processes as he conceives them.

The Golden Bowl is in many ways James's most complex novel. In a Notebook entry for February 14, 1895, James sees his story as a short "international" novel with an "adulterine element" that would disqualify it for Harper's.[27] In his note James talks of the importance of a "narrative plan" and of combining the "narrative" and the "dramatic" elements of his story into a symbiotic union. His ultimate decision for The Golden Bowl, of course, was to do away with the device of the solitary "observer" and to divide the novel into two parts — making the Prince his chief "reflector" in the novel's first half and the Princess in the second. The novel's narrative angle, as James points out in his preface to

The Golden Bowl, is "indirect and oblique" yet "the very straightest and closest possible . . . . [It is] my account of somebody's impression".[28] The latter phrase also perfectly describes the narrative technique of *The Portrait of A Lady,* as I have indicated in preceding pages. Like *The Spoils of Poynton, The Golden Bowl* is a series of meditations, meditations described for the reader by the Jamesian narrator and existing for the most part within the consciousnesses of the two imaginary "reflectors". The subject of each reflector's meditations is almost always the other reflector — that is to say, Maggie Verver is presented to the reader through the Prince's "exhibitory vision" of her throughout the first half of the novel, and then the Prince is presented to the reader in the second half of the novel through his wife's "vision" of him, "the advantage thus being," says James, "that these attributions of experience display the sentient subjects themselves at the same time and by the same stroke with the nearest possible approach to a desirable vividness".[29] Thus the "scheme" of the novel, James says, is that although we "see" very few persons in *The Golden Bowl* (no more than six, and of these only four in detail), "we shall really see as much of them as a coherent literary form permits".[30] Five of the novel's six major characters (we may except Colonel Assingham) are constantly engaged in "seeing about" each other along lines James mentions in "The Art of Fiction", lines that for him constitute "a cluster of gifts" that may "be said to constitute experience": "The power to guess the unseen from the seen, to trace the implication of things, to judge the whole piece by the pattern".[31] Maggie's ability to do exactly this, and Charlotte's failure to do it, are what separate the novel's two "heroines" at the end of the novel, a separation between a theoretical happiness in Europe for Maggie and a theoretical imprisonment in American City for Charlotte. The problem of interpretation, however, is exacerbated by the ambiguity of the ending (a problem I shall examine shortly) and by James's awareness and treatment in this novel and in others, such as *What Maisie Knew, The Sacred Fount,* and *The Wings of the Dove,* of what he calls in "The Art of Fiction" the "traditional difference between that which people know and that which they agree to admit that they know, that which they see and that which they speak of".[32]

A major characteristic of James's style is the use of metaphors of mind which are in effect images of ideas, as we have seen in *The Portrait of A Lady*. In *The Golden Bowl* these metaphors, as I have suggested, are often architectural. I shall devote the remainder of this chapter to an examination of several passages in *The Golden Bowl* (one of which is Maggie's "meditation"), passages which should further help to demonstrate how James's characters think and how the metaphors of mind, especially the architectural ones, are organic to the novel and why they are so consistently employed.

The scene opening Book II of *The Golden Bowl*, in which Maggie Verver meditates at some length about her relationship with her husband, contains an elaborate and extended architectural metaphor which is typical in many ways of the thought-processes of James's characters in this novel. James, even more than George Eliot, draws images from exotic topography and architecture in dramatizing the consciousness of his characters. Maggie's meditation is a case in point.

To reconstruct the scene: *The Golden Bowl* is divided into two books — entitled respectively "The Prince" and "The Princess" — the first of which describes two marriages. Maggie Verver, a rich American, marries an Italian Prince. Maggie's widowed father, at her urging, attempts after his daughter's marriage to evade both loneliness and fortune-hunters by marrying Maggie's old friend Charlotte Stant. Unknown to Maggie and her father, however, is the fact that Charlotte, who is more than twenty years younger than Adam Verver, is also an old acquaintance of the Prince, Maggie's husband. Charlotte and the Prince, in fact, had an affair in Rome several years prior to the present action, and they are still mutually attracted at the time of their marriages to the Ververs — marriages made in part, at least, out of financial necessity. At the end of Book I, Maggie has just begun to realize that her marriage, as well as her father's, may be in jeopardy — for Charlotte and the Prince have become more boldly adulterous after several years of their respective marriages. Book II tells how Maggie, who throughout Book I is virtually incapable of comprehending evil or of acting

positively to defeat it, attempts to "save" both marriages by
confronting her domestic situation realistically and laboring
to alter it. Whether or not she in fact succeeds is debatable,
deliberately left ambiguous at the end of the novel. The
recognition of evil is always a tenuous process, and particularly
so for the innocent Princess. Thus the latter half of *The Golden
Bowl* is especially complex, containing almost no dialogue and
given over for the most part to the analysis of Maggie's psyche.

As Book II opens, the Princess has just begun to realize her
situation and has already taken one or two tentative steps
toward its rectification (miniscule hints to the Prince of her
suspicions). Maggie's meditation is rendered to the reader in
large measure through the medium of metaphor.

It was not till many days had passed that the Princess began to accept
the idea of having done, a little, something she was not always doing, or
indeed that of having listened to any inward voice that spoke in a new
tone. Yet these instinctive postponements of reflection were the fruit,
positively, of recognitions and perceptions already active; of the sense,
above all, that she had made, at a particular hour, made by the mere
touch of her hand, a difference in the situation so long present to her as
practically unattackable. This situation had been occupying, for months
and months, the very centre of the garden of her life, but it had reared
itself there like some strange, tall tower of ivory, or perhaps rather some
wonderful, beautiful, but outlandish pagoda, a structure plated with
hard, bright porcelain, coloured and figured and adorned, at the
overhanging eaves, with silver bells that tinkled, ever so charmingly,
when stirred by chance airs. She had walked round and round it — that
was what she felt; she had carried on her existence in the space left her
for circulation, a space that sometimes seemed ample and sometimes
narrow; looking up, all the while, at the fair structure that spread itself
so amply and rose so high, but never quite making out, as yet, where
she might have entered had she wished. She had not wished till
now — such was the odd case; and what was doubtless equally odd,
besides, was that, though her raised eyes seemed to distinguish
places that must serve, from within, and especially far aloft, as
apertures and outlooks, no door appeared to give access from her
convenient garden level. The great decorated surface had remained
consistently impenetrable and inscrutable. At present, however, to her
considering mind, it was as if she had ceased merely to circle and to
scan the elevation, ceased so vaguely, so quite helplessly to stare and
wonder: she had caught herself distinctly in the act of pausing, then in
that of lingering, and finally in that of stepping unprecedentedly near. The
thing might have been, by the distance at which it kept her, a
Mahometan mosque, with which no base heretic could take a liberty;
there so hung about it the vision of one's putting off one's shoes to
enter, and even, verily, of one's paying with one's life if found there as
an interloper. She had not, certainly, arrived at the conception of

paying with her life for anything she might do; but it was nevertheless quite as if she had sounded with a tap or two one of the rare porcelain plates. She had knocked, in short — though she could scarce have said whether for admission or for what; she had applied her hand to a cool, smooth spot, and waited to see what would happen. Something *had* happened; it was as if a sound, at her touch, after a little, had come back to her from within; a sound sufficiently suggesting that her approach had been noted.[33]

Again the heroine meditates, logically and intelligently, on the subject of her relation to her husband — here, perhaps, more indirectly than in previous meditation scenes. And here, once again, nothing external actually *happens*; Maggie broods over her dilemma, and in doing so begins to clarify in her own mind her position in relation to the Prince. Her slow realization of the evil she must confront and of what will be required of her in this crisis will ultimately enable her to perceive her own position more clearly and thus help her to attempt, at least, to put back together the marriage her husband seems bent on destroying.

The most obvious element of the passage is the metaphorical one, which is emphasized again and again by the typically Jamesian phrase, "it was as if". The basic metaphor is of course architectural; Maggie's conception of her "situation" is expressed in terms of an elaborate ivory tower, an exotic pagoda which becomes in effect the image of an idea, the vision of a vision. James is using a metaphor to define not only a social situation but also a mental experience, and this is a frequent device in fiction in which plot and mental activity are often identical. The encroaching evil in Maggie's domestic situation and the beginning of her reaction to it are projected in an elaborate metaphor which consists, basically, of a pictorial dramatization of consciousness. This is "psychological reality" in a James novel.

The pagoda image, which introduces the Princess as the "center of consciousness" of Book II (it was the Prince in Book I), quite obviously symbolizes Maggie's "situation" itself, "the very centre of the garden of her life".[34] Her slow and hesitating approach, her uncertainty as to what it might contain, typify her indecisiveness, her struggle with an awkward idea, her disinclination to know too much at once. She walks around and around her vision, inspecting it from every angle and occasionally taking some tentative "soundings" of it. Maggie's circling around a stationary object emphasizes something I have already defined as a typical element of James's imagery, something which helps distinguish the mental processes of his characters from those of Meredith's characters. James's protagonists see the situations in which they find themselves in terms of a picture which is a spatial scene that can be brooded on. They see things in terms of other things, confront their images, and then go around them. There always seems to be an element of stasis in their images, as here, for example, the pagoda is the stationary structure around which the Princess walks. There is no corresponding element of stasis in Clara's meditation. The feeling one gets in reading of her thoughts is that of constant and rapid movement, the instantaneous involvement of all her faculties in an organic unity.

The pagoda image is quite obviously Maggie's own image more than it is the narrator's. He, perhaps, selects and organizes to some extent the language in which it is expressed, but the idea itself seems to be primarily her own. It exists in her mind. What the reader encounters in this scene is the narrator's "account" of her "impression", his transmittal of her vision.

This meditation scene, once again, is crucial to the novel's thematic progression. It comes precisely in the center of the novel and marks the beginning of Maggie's emergence from fear and ignorance and the beginning of her new clarity of perception, resulting in a new perspective that will ultimately enable her at least to attempt to find a solution to her conjugal difficulties. She has been blind to these difficulties throughout most of the novel's first half. In the second half of the novel she begins to see them as they really are and to deal with them more effectively. Like Isabel Archer, Maggie is intelligent and articulate but weaker than the combination arrayed against her, in this case that of Charlotte and the Prince. Like Isabel, Maggie is able at least to confront a power stronger than her own in the process of achieving a balance of influences. Maggie's "victory", as the ending of the novel suggests, may perhaps be Pyrrhic, but at least it demonstrates once again that in James's novels, unlike George Eliot's,

stronger wills may sometimes be stymied, through evasion
and strategy, by weaker ones. By the end of the novel Maggie
seems, like Isabel, to have won in the process of losing. That
is to say, she has "saved" both marriages, but the dark
embrace in the novel's final paragraph suggests that her
marriage may be incapable of redemption. After Adam and
Charlotte leave, the Prince turns to Maggie and says, with
his eyes "strangely lighted", that he sees nothing but her.
Maggie, in "pity and dread" of his eyes, "burie[s] her own in
his breast". Maggie has kept her husband, but the stability of
their future life together apparently will be rather precarious.
Perhaps one reason for this ominous note at the end of the
novel is that the stalemate Maggie achieves is, as I have
suggested, a triumph of weakness, an unnatural containment
of strength more powerful than her own.[35]

Keeping the metaphorical structure of Maggie's meditation
in mind, one can see some of the same characteristic imagery
operating throughout other passages in *The Golden Bowl*.
Architectural images as metaphors of mind recur. For example,
Adam Verver's brain is called "a strange workshop of fortune",
a "chamber . . . the windows of which, at hours of highest
pressure, never seemed . . . perceptibly to glow".[36] Even more
impressive is the extended metaphor which describes Adam's
vision of his son-in-law the Prince, a description which lends
itself to comparison with Maggie's meditation in terms of its
metaphorical structure:

At first, certainly, their decent little old-time union, Maggie's and his
own, had resembled a good deal some pleasant public square, in the
heart of an old city, into which a great Palladian church, say — something
with a grand architectural front — had suddenly been dropped; so that
the rest of the place, the space in front, the way round, outside, to the
east end, the margin of street and passage, the quantity of overarching
heaven, had been temporarily compromised. Not even then, of a truth,
in a manner disconcerting — given, that is, for the critical, or at least the
intelligent, eye, the great style of the façade and its high place in its
class . . . . The Palladian church was always there, but the *piazza* took
care of itself. The sun stared down in its fulness, the air circulated, and
the public not less; the limit stood off, the way round was easy, the
east end was as fine, in its fashion, as the west, and there were also side
doors for entrance, between the two — large, monumental, ornamental,
in *their* style — as for all proper great churches. By some such process,
in fine, had the Prince, for his father-in-law, while remaining solidly a
feature, ceased to be, at all ominously, a block . . . . It figured for him,

clearly, as a final idea, a conception of the last vividness. He might
have been signifying by it the sharp corners and hard edges, all the stony
pointedness, the grand right geometry of his spreading Palladian church.
Just so, he was insensible to no feature of the felicity of a contact that,
beguilingly, almost confoundingly, was a contact but with practically
yielding lines and curved surfaces.[37]

Clearly, this vision is principally Adam's own and exists in
his mind, just as the pagoda image exists in Maggie's mind.[38]
The narrator gives his "account" of Adam's "impression",
but the impression, the vision, belongs for the most part to
Adam himself. The narrator merely selects and organizes the
language in which Adam's mental picture is expressed. Maggie
sees her relationship to the Prince in terms of an exotic ivory
tower; her father sees his relationship to his son-in-law in
terms of a Palladian church. The literal fact of the Prince's
intrusion upon the relationship between Adam and his
daughter — an intrusion Adam has learned how to bear
without feeling offended — is expressed not literally but rather
in terms of a vision Adam has of his idea of the Prince. The
oblique view — the vision of a vision — is the usual one in
James's novels. Adam, who later on thinks of his daughter as a
Greek statue, has the habit generally of thinking of people as
objects — a "trick", James calls it in an aside, "mainly of his
own mind". James's people, as I have been suggesting,
constantly see things analogically. The scenes and people they
encounter are incarnated in their minds in the form of pictures
of other things. Once again, at the center of this mental image
is a stationary object that is exhaustively scrutinized by the
character thinking. Adam encounters his own idea and then
circles around it, inspecting his Palladian church from every
angle. Like Maggie, he broods on what is essentially a
metaphorical reconstruction of the original object of interest.
  Adam's dawning consciousness of his loneliness after
Maggie's marriage and of Maggie's desire to see him married
in his turn is described in terms remarkably similar to those
employed to illuminate Maggie's slowly growing awareness of
her own marital situation: "he had knocked at the door of
that essentially private house [his own mind], and his call, in
truth, had not been immediately answered; so that when, after
waiting and coming back, he had at last got in, it was . . . as a

thief at night".[39] Just as Maggie knocks tentatively at one of
the "rare porcelain plates" of her pagoda, so Adam, pictured
here as knocking at the door of his own mind, takes the first
step toward revelation through self-examination. The answer
he seeks, like the answers she seeks, seem to be located behind
the walls of a metaphorical building, walls which may well
represent barriers imposed on the human mind by its own
failures to see, to examine things, to cultivate understanding.
James was always arguing for this sort of expansion, and the
obstacles on the way to it were usually, he seemed to feel, of
human construction. Thus the act of scaling the walls finally
becomes, by extension, an emblem for the dissipation of
self-imposed blindness.

Once again, the image used to describe the process of
mental exploration is architectural. James, as a matter of
fact, underlines the appropriateness of using such language
to describe Adam's mental activity by telling the reader that
Adam's face "somewhat resembled a small, decent room,
clean-swept and unencumbered with furniture, but drawing a
particular advantage . . . from the outlook of a pair of ample
and uncurtained windows".[40]

The image of Adam Verver as a housebreaker violating his
own mind is repeated in part in a later passage relating the
metaphor to the Princess. Maggie admits to herself that the
unanswered questions she has had about her husband are
"like a roomful of confused objects, never as yet 'sorted',
which for some time she had been passing and re-passing along
the corridors of her life. She passed it when she could without
opening the door; then, on occasion, she turned the
key . . . . She, at present, by a mental act, once more pushed
the door open".[41] This passage follows by just a few pages the
pagoda metaphor, and repeats the image of Maggie's dilemma
as a building, her own apprehension of her "situation" as an
architectural edifice that must be penetrated, or at least
encountered, before knowledge can be attained.

Maggie sees herself, finally, toying with Fanny Assingham's
interest in her affairs like "a mischievous child, playing on the
floor, [piling] up blocks, skilfully and dizzily, with an eye on
the face of a covertly-watching elder. When the blocks
tumbled down they but acted after the nature of blocks; yet

the hour would come for their rising so high that the structure would have to be noticed and admired".[42]

Thus a basic quality of characters' thoughts in *The Golden Bowl* is once again their metaphorical nature, and the metaphors of mind employed are often architectural. The question finally arises: Why do James's characters think so often in terms of architectural images? James uses such metaphors consistently throughout his work, as my discussion of *The Golden Bowl* confirms.[43] In his addiction to metaphors of houses, James had what could only be called an edifice complex. In his essays he frequently speaks of fiction as "the house of fiction" and of the artist as though he were an architect or a builder of literary edifices.[44] In his novels, James often constructs metaphorical houses for his pretentious, unperceptive, or self-deluded protagonists; their houses and their gardens, like many of those in Dickens's novels, are frequently made to represent themselves in some way. The metaphoric buildings usually also suit the characters who dream of them, just as the literal houses people actually live in in James's novels often take on the characteristics of their owners or inhabitants. The most famous example of this is of course Osmond's villa in *The Portrait of A Lady*. In the usual James novel, then, things often acquire a symbolic significance of some kind, a significance that renders, in part, the nature and plight of the characters themselves. Madame Merle in *The Portrait* puts it this way: " 'I've a great respect for things! One's self — for other people — is one's expression of one's self; and one's house, one's furniture, one's garments, the books one reads, the company one keeps — these things are all expressive' ".[45] Now Madam Merle is one of the villains of *The Portrait*, but there can be little doubt that in the foregoing passage she is speaking with James's voice.

The house metaphors, then, are employed to help delineate the characters with whom they are associated. They represent and reflect the psychic nature of the person thinking of them. In *The Golden Bowl* Maggie's "education" — her quest for knowledge — is figured in a house image. A typical example of the unperceptive, innocent Jamesian heroine, she finally desires to know, late in the novel, the innermost rooms, the skeletons in the closet, the family ghosts, as it were. The edifice in her thoughts is an edifice of education, of self-scrutiny, of increasing self-knowledge and ultimate revelation. Its walls represent barriers to comprehension which must be gotten over. Thus the acquisition of objective perception, the learning of the art of vision, is likened by James to the exploration of houses. This may also be because the "situations" in which the characters often find themselves in *The Golden Bowl* are of human construction, things put together (as opposed to things natural), works, almost, of art, like the novel itself, and therefore appropriately symbolized as rare and exotic buildings.

IV

James's people, in *The Portrait of A Lady, The Golden Bowl,* and often elsewhere, do not, in sum, think of each other or of other things directly; the direction of their thoughts is less linear than it is circular or triangular. Y does not think of Z directly, without intermediary, but rather in terms of X. Such a mode of thought is perhaps appropriate for people who often shrink from direct physical encounters as well as personal and private revelations, people who on the one hand rarely exhibit sensual passion and on the other arrive at knowledge of themselves only after tortuous mental gymnastics. Isabel and Maggie both manage to elude an understanding of their "situations" for a long period of time; the habit of circuitous cogitation therefore becomes perfectly appropriate to their psychic structures and also becomes a source of irony for the reader, whose own perception of what is going on is more direct because of the narrator's total vision. It is likely that James himself was in some ways the same sort of person as I have been defining here, and indeed personal anecdotes of his later years, as well as his later novels, testify to the orotundity and indirectness of his thinking.[46] It is known, too, that James did not write his later novels in longhand, but rather dictated them to a secretary, a source, it may be, of primary indirection at the outset. Thus James's style, as I said at the beginning of this chapter, is both metaphorical and indirect — or perhaps, more precisely, metaphorical *because* indirect. People who can identify things only by thinking of them as being like something else must inevitably think in terms of images. Such an explanation should help us to understand why James's people think the way they do and why, in fact, James writes the way he does. His imagination, in all probability, was very much like the imaginations of his characters, the nature of which I have been attempting to define here. His characters must recast what is outside of themselves before they can see within. Epistemologically, at least, the directions of their thoughts are clearly denoted. For James, a person must understand object before he can understand subject. But he will rarely experience object literally or physically, as George Eliot's characters usually do. Instead he will tend more often to experience his surroundings metaphorically, constantly incarnating experience into picture. Thus while Clara Middleton can rationalize out of existence her feeling of bodily imprisonment, Isabel Archer cannot — for the prison exists as an image within her mind and stays with her. There is literal oppression in James's world, of course, but his characters tend to extrapolate from it a further and more suffocating metaphorical oppression. They are able to explain to themselves the meaning or nature of something only by magnifying it into something other than that which it actually is. After understanding a thing in this way, they are then ready to discover its relationship to themselves — what it means to and for them. Revelation takes place first "outside" and then "inside", although of course the process of exterior apprehension necessarily involves the intellect. This formula reverses Meredith's system, in which one sees out only after his own being has been totally revealed to himself. James and Meredith are alike, however, in employing so often the method of dramatic representation, a device requisite to convey to the reader the sense each writer has of the complex intricacy of the human mental processes.

[1] James's pieces on George Eliot include the following items: a review of *Felix Holt* in the *Nation* and an article entitled "The Novels of George Eliot" in the *Atlantic* in 1866; a two-part review of *The Spanish Gypsy* (poems) in the *Nation* in 1868; a review of *Middlemarch* in *Galaxy* in 1873; a review of *The Legend of Jubal* (poems) in the *Nation* in 1874; "*Daniel Deronda*: A Conversation" in the *Atlantic* in 1876; a review of some of George Eliot's shorter stories in the

Nation in 1878; an article entitled "The Life of George Eliot" in the *Atlantic* in 1885; and a chapter on George Eliot in *The Middle Years* (1917), the third and last volume of his uncompleted autobiography. This is more than James wrote on any other writer, unless one considers his book and three essays on Hawthorne. But in terms of number of items devoted to a single writer, George Eliot leads with nine, followed by Howells with six and Balzac with five.

[2] Henry James, *The Future of the Novel*, ed. Leon Edel (1956), p.82.

[3] ibid., p. 83.

[4] ibid., p. 87.

[5] See "Isabel, Gwendolen, and Dorothea", *ELH*, XXX (1963), 144-157.

[6] F.O. Matthiessen and Kenneth B. Murdock (eds.), *The Notebooks of Henry James* (1947), p. 15.

[7] Professor Levine makes some of these same points in his excellent article.

[8] See Chapter 4, n. 11.

[9] See Mrs. Leavis's pungent article, "A Note on Literary Indebtedness: Dickens, George Eliot, Henry James", in the *Hudson Review*, VIII (1955), 423-428.

[10] Morris Shapira (ed.), *Selected Literary Criticism of Henry James* (1964), pp. 36-45, *passim*. The "Conversation" has been reprinted widely. F.R. Leavis, for example, appended it to *The Great Tradition*.

[11] ibid., p. 45.

[12] ibid., p. 46.

[13] ibid., pp. 36-44, *passim*.

[14] ibid., p. 46.

[15] ibid., p. 41.

[16] Most of James's prefaces have been collected and appear in *The Art of the Novel*, ed. R.P.Blackmur (1934). The Preface to *The Portrait of A Lady* appears on pp. 40-58. Most of the quotations in the present paragraph appear on pp. 49-51.

[17] Several other critics have dwelt on the relationship between *Daniel Deronda* and *The Portrait of A Lady*. Some examples are Oscar Cargill, " 'The Portrait of A Lady': A Critical Reappraisal", *Modern Fiction Studies*, III (1957), 11-32, who argues that Osmond is derived from Grandcourt but that Gwendolen and Isabel are quite different; and Cornelia Pulsifer Kelley, *The Early Development of Henry James* (1965), pp. 293-295, who argues that Isabel and Osmond are copies of Gwendolen and Grandcourt. The earliest, longest, and most interesting treatment of the subject is that by F.R. Leavis in *The Great Tradition*, pp. 85-118. Leavis flatly states that James could not have written *The Portrait of A Lady* without first reading *Daniel Deronda*. "Isabel Archer is Gwendolen and Osmond is Grandcourt", he says; "Isabel Archer is Gwendolen Harleth seen by a man . . . . Osmond so plainly *is* Grandcourt, hardly disguised, that the general derivative relation of James's novel to George Eliot's becomes quite unquestionable". The rest of Leavis's discussion is devoted to the argument that *Daniel Deronda*, or at least the "Gwendolen Harleth half" of it, is superior to anything in James's novel. Leavis accuses James of "idealizing", which translates "not seeing", and the result, says Leavis, is that *The Portrait* is "immeasurably less real". James, says Leavis, "admired George Eliot's inwardness and completeness of rendering", but "the difference between [them] is largely a matter of what he leaves out". Thus the "weakness" in *The Portrait*, concludes Leavis, results in large measure because James "derives so much more from George Eliot than he suspects".

[18] See Chapter 4, n. 2.

[19] I am quoting from the Anchor paperback edition of *What Maisie Knew* (1954), p. 150.

[20] *The Future of the Novel*, p. 21. "The Art of Fiction" has also been reprinted widely — e.g., in Morris Shapira's selective collection of James's essays cited in n. 10, above.

[21] ibid., p. 29.

[22] See n.16, above.

[23] *The Portrait of A Lady*, Volume III, Chapter 3, pp. 29-45, *passim.*, in the Macmillan Edition of James's works. This and the New York Edition are the two standard editions of James's works, the major difference between them being, of course, that the New York Edition includes James's later revisions of his novels, while the Macmillan Edition does not. I am using the Macmillan Edition of *The Portrait* for purposes of citation, but I have incorporated James's later revisions of the novel into the passages just quoted. James's revisions of *The Portrait* have been fairly widely discussed, perhaps most intelligently and at some length by F.O. Matthiessen in an appendix to his study, *Henry James: The Major Phase* (1944), pp. 152-186.

   Between the first two sections of the meditation quoted in the text I have omitted only a few words. Between the second and third sections I have left out two long paragraphs in which Isabel recalls to herself how much she had been charmed by Osmond during their courtship, begins to see that her money was a contributing factor to her present woe, and concludes that she married Osmond while laboring under the "factitious theory" of his being "better than anyone else". Between the third and fourth sections I have omitted several sentences in which Isabel admits to herself that her husband treats her opinions and ideas with total scorn.

[24] It is the theme, for example, of *Daisy Miller* (1878) and a cluster of James's "international" stories and *nouvelles*, as well as an important element of *The American* (1877), *The Ambassadors* (1903), and some of his other novels.

[25] It is also raised in *The Golden Bowl*, as I shall demonstrate shortly.

[26] See Chapter 3, n.9. Professor Stallman concentrates his discussion of architectural imagery on *The Portrait of A Lady* and makes an excellent case for its presence in that novel, but he totally neglects *The Golden Bowl*, which, I think, provides a much better example of James's penchant for architectural metaphors.

[27] *The Notebooks of Henry James*, pp. 187-188.

[28] *The Art of the Novel*, p. 327.

[29] ibid., p. 330.

[30] ibid.

[31] *The Future of the Novel*, p. 13.

[32] ibid., p. 25.

[33] *The Golden Bowl*, Volume II, Book II, pp. 3-5 in the New York Edition. All further quotations from *The Golden Bowl* are taken from this edition. There has been by and large no full-scale attempt among James's critics thus far to anatomize the pagoda image and see what it means, but some writers have inevitably noticed the image and hurled various adjectives at it in passing. F.R. Leavis perhaps represents those who are repelled by James's later style when he says that the pagoda image epitomizes the "synthetic and analytical" aspects of the later novels as over against the "imaginative and poetic" imagery of James's earlier fiction (*The Great Tradition*, p. 167). One must make allowances for Mr. Leavis, whose favorite James novel after *The Portrait of A Lady* is *The Awkward Age*. On the other hand, those who find the later novels more to their taste sometimes

tersely cite the pagoda image by way of illustration, though never with much accompanying explanation or analysis. Thus Joseph Warren Beach, in *The Method of Henry James*, first published, remarkably enough, in 1918, says that the pagoda metaphor typifies, in its evocation of Maggie's domestic situation, the "dark and lustrous splendor" of James's later novels; Stephen Spender, in *The Destructive Element* (1936),comments on the "dream imagery" of the later novels and says that "it is natural that a James character should not think in terms of phalluses, but of ivory towers, beautiful lakes, pagodas, and golden bowls" (p. 83); F.O. Matthiessen, in *Henry James: The Major Phase*, calls the pagoda image "dazzling"; Leon Edel, in *The Psychological Novel 1900-1950* (1955), calls the passage typical of the "symbolist poetry" of James's later period (see especially pp. 187-188); and R.P. Blackmur, in his introduction to the Dell paperback edition of *The Golden Bowl* (1963), cites the pagoda image as one typical of James's later style in its evocation of the "actions of the human psyche".

[34] There is a sense, perhaps, in which one may view the pagoda as being an oblique representation of the Prince himself. Its carefully described shape makes the pagoda seem vaguely, rather ornamentally, phallic. This would be in keeping with James's characterization of the Prince, who is both an elegant anomaly and a symbol of virility in the novel. But the paramount meaning of the pagoda metaphor is, I think, as I go on to define it in the text of this discussion — that is, as a representation of Maggie's "situation", of which the Prince is of course a central element.

[35] R.P. Blackmur, in his introduction to the Dell edition of *The Golden Bowl*, goes even further. The novel, he says, ultimately "repudiates" human behavior. Maggie Verver is an Iago who ruins everybody's lives, the Prince is a tragic hero, and the destruction of life, concludes Mr. Blackmur, is a theme repeated throughout all of James's late fiction. This view, I think, is rather extravagant, but it is fairly close to those of F.R. Leavis in *The Great Tradition*, who says (p. 160) that the reader's sympathies in *The Golden Bowl* lie solely with Charlotte and the Prince, and R.W.B. Lewis in *The American Adam* (1955), who emphasizes (p. 154) the "cruelty of innocence" in the novel.

[36] Vol. I, Book I, p.128.

[37] ibid., pp. 136-139, *passim*.

[38] As James got older he tended to conceive of the mental processes of human beings as being more subject to images and visions (and perhaps was more subject to them himself), and thus while his earlier heroes and heroines think quite often in metaphors (as Isabel Archer does, for example), they do not do so as consistently as the protagonists of the later novels. Lambert Strether and Milly Theale in *The Ambassadors* and *The Wings of the Dove* are just two examples outside of *The Golden Bowl*. Christopher Newman, the protagonist of *The American*, a novel written twenty-five years before the trio of great last novels, thinks for the most part in literal and uncircuitous language.

[39] Vol. I, Book I, p.151.

[40] ibid, p. 173.

[41] Vol. II, Book II, p. 15. The reader's attention may be recalled at this point to Dorothea in *Middlemarch*, whose "vistas" are "replaced by anterooms and winding passages which . . . lead nowhither".

[42] ibid., pp. 106-107.

[43] Architectural images, as I have said previously, are present to some extent too in *The Portrait of A Lady*, but I have ignored them for the most part in my discussion of that novel in the interest of further elucidating the particular pattern that has been my focus in this study, and also because Professor Stallman has, I think, covered the architectural ground in *The Portrait* quite admirably. See Chapter 3, n. 9, and n. 26, above.

[44] Just one salient example is a long passage in the preface to *The Portrait of A Lady* which begins thus: "The house of fiction has . . . not one window, but a million — a number of possible windows not to be reckoned, rather; every one of which has been pierced, or is still pierceable, in its vast front, by the need of the individual vision and by the pressure of the individual will".

[45] Vol. I, Chapter 19, p.190.

[46] One well-known and rather sadly amusing example of James's inability to speak in clear and direct terms in his later years is recounted at some length by Edith Wharton in her autobiography. See *A Backward Glance* (1933), pp. 241-243.